Equipped
for Change

Doing the Deep Work
of Transformation

KEISHA A. RIVERS, M.Ed.

SPARK Publications
Charlotte, North Carolina

Equipped for Change:
Doing the Deep Work of Transformation
Keisha A. Rivers, M.Ed.

Designed, produced, and published by
SPARK Publications
SPARKpublications.com
Charlotte, North Carolina

Excerpt from *The Choice* by Og Mandino is used with
permission from Penguin Random House.

Cover art by Ninja Artist/Shutterstock.com,
Valerie Johnson/Shutterstock.com, and Andrey Yurlov/
Shutterstock.com with photo illustration
by SPARK Publications

Softcover, December 2020, ISBN: 978-1-953555-03-8
Library of Congress Control Number: 2020923597

This book is the result of a journey of discovery and reflection. Each person that I have encountered has left their mark on my development and has contributed to this moment. Thank you for being in the right place at the right time.

This book is dedicated to those who have poured into me, believed in me, supported me, and walked alongside me. I also dedicate this book to those who are traveling on their own journey of change. Don't give up. Don't turn back. The world needs you.

Table of Contents

PART I
The Process of Change: Don't Take It Personally; Make It Personal

PART II
The Deep Work of Change: Transforming Organizations from the Inside Out

Before We Begin

Before we begin, there's something you should know: I never intended to write this book.

I mean, I intended to write *a* book titled *Equipped for Change*, but it had a very different purpose and a much different feel. That book was designed to provide companies with tools, insights, and strategies on how to get the best out of their people by equipping them to deal with change. That book was written for companies and organizations, not for people. Even though that book was about equipping people, it was still organization focused. The perspective was what organizations needed to learn to better care for their people during change, so they could achieve more, be more successful, and help contribute to the company's bottom line.

But writing that book somehow didn't "feel" right. I started and stopped, revised, and rethought the contents of that book for months. I knew that the pieces were right—people, organizations, and change—but the emphasis and the order was somehow "off" for me. Then something happened.

COVID-19 reared its ugly head and completely crashed the world as we knew it—I mean crashed *everything* across the entire globe! Whole countries shut down, global travel came to a halt, and business as we knew it shifted overnight. Companies had to pivot to focus on how to care for their employees because they finally realized that the well-being of their people was of utmost importance. No longer was work-life balance a fringe consideration; it became the main discussion. People were at home, during a pandemic, trying to work. They were not simply working from home. (That's if they were working at all.)

And as if that wasn't enough to deal with, a little over four months into this shift, in the midst of a global pandemic, George Floyd was murdered in Minneapolis when a White police officer kneeled on his neck for eight minutes and forty-six seconds. Mr. Floyd was suffocated in broad daylight on a public street with a crowd gathered around and people filming it. The entire time he kneeled on George Floyd's neck, the police officer seemed unconcerned, unbothered, and kept one hand in his pocket while the man beneath his knee literally cried and begged for his life as he realized he was dying. When the video was released, it seemed as if the world exploded. People were horrified at the callous disregard for human life—for a Black man's life. Overnight, a spotlight was shined on long-standing issues of discrimination, police brutality, systemic racism, and the experiences of Black people in America and across the globe.

In the midst of the protests, civil unrest, and widespread shifts in what was once known as "normal," a new focus arose for businesses and organizations. For the first time in a long time, companies had to pivot and not just appease their employees. They had to focus on what their employees actually needed. Additionally, they had to step up with immediate action and follow through, not just to ride the wave, but to create long-term, sustainable change.

So here we are. The book I was going to write is no longer relevant. But the book that you are holding in your hands is exactly what is needed in this time, on this day, and beyond. It is no longer a book about how to guide organizations in how to get the most out of their people by equipping them to embrace and manage change. Instead, this book is written to *equip people* to navigate, embrace, and *lead* the process of change and transformation in systems and organizations.

Books like this are sometimes viewed as an attempt to tell people what to do, or maybe even to prop up the author as some kind of "know it all" expert to be revered and worshiped as being the one with all the answers. Well, I hate to disappoint you—well, actually, I'm happy to disappoint you—that isn't what this book is about. My reason for writing this book was to share my journey and the processes that I have discovered along the way. My purpose in sharing my personal journey is to create an opportunity for you to pause and maybe think a bit differently about your own process. I wrote this book because I simply wanted to help. I wanted to make sure that I could prevent others from struggling through the process of change the way I used to. I wanted to keep you from having to go through this journey alone. I wanted to share my story so that you would see for yourself that you can do it too.

This isn't a typical business book. It's not completely written in "professionalese" as I call it. It's not filled with case studies, references to published articles, or expert opinions. While I don't include the proof of concept from my work with clients in this book, I didn't omit them because I didn't see them as being noteworthy or important. Rather, I chose instead to take this approach because I wanted you to understand intellectually and feel me personally.

Change is a process that begins with an event. If organizations want to be successful, there has to be a shift in management, leadership, and processes that focuses on how to do the most with *all* of your people in order to succeed as a *result* of your people.

Change is a personal process. No matter what the setting or the outcome, it affects each of us personally and deeply. Change is integral to our sense of who we are as individuals. Every time we go through an experience that shakes our foundations and rattles the core of who we think we are and what we think we know, it causes us to take pause. There is no such thing as a separation of professional and personal. Who you are personally informs and impacts your professional life, and who you are professionally impacts your personal life. The two are intertwined. I needed to show you through my experience how the two connect and influence each other, so you would be open to embracing that aspect of the journey for yourself.

I am a notoriously private person, so sharing so much of my Hurricane Katrina experience was something I didn't take lightly. In fact, I actually agonized over it and tried to come up with so many different reasons why I shouldn't share it so prominently in this book. Once I realized that I *had* to tell that story in detail if I wanted to take you along this journey, the only issue became just how much to share. I'm not telling you that you have to share all of your deepest secrets with the whole world as part of this process, but I am encouraging you to consider sharing more of yourself and your journey with those closest to you. You have an enormous amount of influence on those in your circle. Most times the opportunity to encourage others or even to allow them to support you or learn vicariously through your experience is lost because you want to remain closed off to protect yourself. If I can do it, you can do it.

In this book, I will discuss the process of changing systems, having difficult and necessary conversations, and effectively dealing with and dismantling issues that are barriers to creating truly diverse, inclusive, equitable learning environments where people are centered in the work and integral to overall success.

I wrote this book for those who desire to be change agents — people who are leaders, aspiring leaders, managers, supervisors, and team members within their organizations, those who see an opportunity for change and who have a desire to help spark and guide change within their circles of influence. Having a passion and desire for change is great. Understanding the process of change so that you can effectively navigate, manage, and embrace it is even better. I like this book much better. I think you will too.

Finally, I want to thank you. Thank you for picking up this book and believing it to be interesting and insightful enough to dedicate your time and effort to read. Time is our most precious gift, and the fact that you chose to spend some of it with me means the world to me. I am deeply humbled and forever grateful to you in sharing this journey with me and for being open to learning, so you can share your journey with others.

Keisha Rivers

First Things First

If you and I are going to be spending some time together as you read this book, we need to come to a meeting of the minds on a few things.

First of all, I'm not a "stuffy professional." I write as I speak because I want you to get to know me and connect with me. To do that, you need to see and hear *me*. If you want to understand me, you'll need to know some things about me that I'll reveal as we go along.

Secondly, I believe in the power of words and the importance of language and meaning. I understand that language has memory, and because the words that I choose have a past and history with you already, I need to make sure that we're operating from the same shared meaning when I say things. To help with this process, I'll lay some foundations in language, meaning, nuances, mindset, etc., as I go along.

Third, I am an educator by passion, training, and profession. Because of this, I have a strong belief and commitment to providing space for learning, growth, and development. I don't believe in the "empty vessel" model where you would be considered empty of all knowledge, background, and skills and where it is my job to "pour" into you and fill you up with what I brought to the table. Nope. Not me. I believe in a constructivist model where you already come with a wealth of knowledge, information, perspectives, and experience, and you use that along with what I share to create or construct your new ways of thinking, being, and doing. In short—you're gonna have to do the work if you wanna reap the rewards. Sorry … not sorry.

Lastly, I ask a lot of questions, and I love telling stories. I'm a creative, so I love painting pictures and exploring concepts and ideas. I enjoy questioning, reflecting, and taking deep dives into the process and your progress during our journey together. I feel that the more real I can make this for you, the better you'll connect and the more successful you'll become.

The format and flow of this book can serve as a model for you in how to work with your own teams and colleagues in doing this work. If you decide to take this route, let me give you a couple words of caution: 1) Don't beat yourself up. It takes concerted effort and lots of practice for this approach to become second nature if you're not used to it already. 2) Don't try to imitate me. You can use this as a guide, and there will be examples, questions, and suggestions for questions, approaches, and strategies that you can use, but these don't work unless you and everyone involved bring your whole, authentic selves to the process. If you're bringing all of *you* to this process, then you can't do it trying to be like me.

I'm so excited about your willingness to learn, grow, and do your part as a change agent and change facilitator in your circle of influence. Trying something new isn't always people's first choice, so when I come across people like you who are willing to put in the work and do the heavy lifting of change, it makes me do my happy dance!

Now that I've gotten that out of the way, I want to actually introduce myself. You may have read some of my bio already, heard me speak at an event, or listened to my *Mindset 2 Mastery* podcast and therefore have some idea about my personality and how I roll. But if you don't, or even if you do, I wanted to share some things about me that will help us get to know each other along this journey.

I grew up in Mount Pleasant, South Carolina. At the time, it was a relatively lesser-known town across the bridge from its larger neighbor, Charleston. (Today, there are *way* too many people who know about it, if the traffic, increased population, and major development are any indication. But, hey, that's just my opinion as someone who misses the pristine beaches and undisturbed nature trails of my youth.) Growing up as a Black girl in South Carolina was an experience that helped to prepare me at an early age for the work that I do today.

Professionally, I have spent the past three decades working on and involved in various aspects of organizational change. I have been active in organizing, managing, and facilitating professional organizations; leading strategic planning and development retreats; creating curriculum and development materials; leading learning sessions; designing and conducting leadership development programs; creating and leading business development series; and speaking, coaching, and consulting. My focus has always been on creating opportunities for learning, growth, and development.

Because I spent so much of my life fighting for change and cultivating opportunities for dialogue, development, and collaboration, this work is innate. It is an integral part of who I am and shows up in the way in which I move through the world. It is my hope that through this journey, you will find your own voice and create your own path to embracing, navigating, and being equipped as an agent for change.

What Is Change?

Change exposes the cracks in the armor and the kinks in the system. It highlights and shines a light upon discrimination, disparities, and differences.

Change magnifies your shortcomings and exposes your weaknesses. It jolts you unceremoniously out of your comfort zone and forces you to address uncomfortable issues as it reveals the truth of long-standing lies.

Change is impartial. It equally reveals the best—and the worst—within people, organizations, systems, and processes.

Change reveals the truth most people need but are unwilling to see.

Change presents opportunities for creativity and innovation. It forces reflection, assessment, and honest evaluation to continue your journey of growth.

Change is the only thing that is constant in our lives. It lives with us, shapes us, challenges us, and cultivates growth in us. Change is the reason we are who we are and become who we become.

Change is more than a set of steps and plans. It is a process of transformation that forces a shift in the thinking and mindset of your people. To be effective and sustainable, change requires building a new foundation and making new connections.

Change is *messy*. No matter how much you prepare for it and understand the process of it, you will still feel uncomfortable and, in most cases, unprepared. And to be honest, that is the point. Moving into a "next normal" on the other side of change requires you to go through a process that moves you out of your comfort zone and places you on a new path. Because people as a whole crave the familiar, it will be necessary for you to consciously embrace the discomfort as you travel the path of growth and come out better on the other side. Learn to sit with it, reflect upon it, and accept it for what it is.

Change is always, always, *always* personal. No matter the setting or purpose of change, there will be emotion, connections, and triggers. The people side of change needs to amplify the voices, stories, and experiences of those involved in the process. All stakeholders must be heard. You can only manage the process of change effectively if you consider the impact on you and your people as individuals.

But as is so often true with us as individuals and within organizations, we do not look at change as a constant, necessary thing that is actually good for us. We see change as a disruption—something to avoid and fear. With that perspective, it is no wonder that we are caught off guard when faced with change events and push back against making adjustments that will take us out of our comfort zones.

This book is the beginning of you taking ownership of that process and shifting the narrative. Unless you, your team, and your organization begin changing your mindset about change, you will continue to be overwhelmed by it and lose out on opportunities to become better and more successful as a result of it.

What to Expect

To truly understand and become equipped for change, you must begin by understanding the process of change. You will hear me say repeatedly that "change is a process that begins with an event." (I tend to repeat things that are important, so get used to it.) So often people spend most of their time focusing on the event that they miss the process and fail to do the work necessary to bring about lasting change, which is, in effect, creating their "next normal." When people skip the process of change and fail to do the work, they end up repeating the same cycle of reacting, resolving to "do better," and then falling back into something that feels and looks eerily similar to what used to be before the event. (Cue the saying, "Oh, they're always trying something new, but just wait awhile, and they'll go back to doing things the old way soon enough.")

The process of change involves three steps: (1) the catalyst (event), (2) the shift (transformation), and (3) the next normal (application). If you skip any of the steps in the process, you cannot hope to lead and create lasting, sustainable, and successful change in people, organizations, and systems.

Throughout this book, I will examine each of the steps in the process; discuss examples of what each step looks like in action; outline strategies and questions to ask; and identify ways to implement change with your team and organization. Consider this an interactive journey where you will be asked to reflect upon your own thinking process, examine your tendencies, and create new steps for action. I am not going to tell you exactly what to do. Instead, my goal is to equip you with the tools to help you make decisions and honor them with action on your own journey.

Since you're more than likely reading this book because you're in charge of or part of an organization going through change (or needs to), I will also examine change from an organization's perspective, specifically how you can better equip yourself for change in the context of engagement, learning, and leadership. There are other areas that can be explored, but for the sake of time, I'll focus on these three. I believe they are the key elements in creating dynamic people-centered organizations that can achieve specific outcomes and create long-term, sustainable success.

Even though you may be reading this book to assist you in gaining the insights and tools necessary to positively impact your team or organization, I want you to think about this as a personal journey of discovery, growth, and learning. Remember: change is always, always, *always* personal. Each team or organization is only as strong and successful as the people in it. If we all take responsibility for our personal growth and development, then naturally when we come together, we will create better teams and stronger organizations.

In this process, it is important to share your stories, reflections, thoughts, and experiences. Each person has a voice and brings value through their active participation. Again, I do not subscribe to the "empty vessel" model where people wait to be "filled" with information provided by an expert. I understand that you already bring a wealth of information, insights, and experiences to the table. It is through tapping into this individual wealth that you can bring out the best in your teams, groups, and organizations. So in this model, I focus on constructing new knowledge and creating new paradigms that will engage and equip you and your people not simply to follow a script of behaviors or skills, but rather to think and respond effectively based on the situation and the circumstances facing you. Because of this approach, you should plan to maintain a journal and portfolio of your thoughts and work that chronicles your process and showcases your progress.

A final note: the work of change is transformational. No one can do a deep dive into what it means to personally participate in the process of change without coming out different on the other side. The goal *is* for you to be transformed. If you only go through the motions, then it will be extremely difficult to experience any breakthroughs. Vulnerability and transparency are not only key but also required. Change is not a process you can pay lip service to. There is no way you can be all talk and not be expected to walk that talk.

Because change is fundamentally a personal process, I begin this book by examining the process of change through a personal lens in part I. In part II, I expand the focus from the individual to include the organization. In that section, we'll discuss how to navigate the journey of change while participating in the process of the deep work of change necessary to transform organizations and systems. Keep in mind that even though these two aspects of change are addressed in two separate parts of this book, they are interconnected. Consider part I to be a building block of part II. You cannot do the deep work of transforming organizations if you do not do the deep work of transforming yourself.

Now that the foundation has been set, let us begin.

"You cannot do
the deep work
of transforming
organizations if you do
not do the deep work of
transforming yourself."

The Process of Change: Don't Take It Personally; Make It Personal

CHAPTER 1

Preparing for Change

Preparing for change isn't about having a crystal ball or being able to predict the future. It doesn't have anything to do with having a perfect plan, but it does involve thinking ahead, laying a foundation, and being able to adjust and adapt to situations and circumstances that will equip you to handle whatever comes your way. The steps in the process of change are the same for everyone, but the situations surrounding that process are different. Everyone reacts to change events differently. Everyone responds to stress in various ways. Everyone has a different personality and perspective on the way they show up in the world. The way you think about change and the way you prepare for change is a huge determining factor in how you navigate change.

As I sit half-listening to the news program playing in the background, I can't help but think about the "what ifs" racing through my mind. What if I had decided to leave sooner? What if I had actually taken that job offer and moved out of state forty-five days ago? What if I had registered the inherent danger in the fact that looking UP at a cruise ship traveling slowly next to me on the Mississippi River meant I was actually standing several feet BELOW sea level (eight feet to be exact)—something my brain just didn't seem to be able to compute.

After all, who actually registers what it means to live in a city eight feet below sea level anyway? Nobody realizes that living in a bowl below the level of the water around you spells trouble. All those times when the streets flooded after an afternoon thunderstorm. The times when the pumping stations threatened to overflow, struggling to keep up with the rapid rainfall during the rainy season. The times I shook off any worries about my safety by assuring myself that we hadn't experienced any major damage in, well, forever—so naturally we were okay, weren't we?

What if we, as a community, had lobbied harder for improvements? What if we had paid more attention to the threats that we barely escaped every single storm season? What if, what if, what if?

Well, I didn't take heed to any of those warnings. I hadn't made any different decisions or significantly altered my standard routine of advanced preparations. I hadn't trusted my instincts and that tingling on the back of my neck that told me over and over again that there was something to pay attention to here.

So here I am. Sitting in my living room with the windows boarded up, listening to the rain pounding on the roof outside, halfway drowning out the sound of the same facts being repeated over and over again on the news about the impending storm. The what ifs tumble over each other as I am left to wait. There is nothing else to do.

When in the midst of a change event, it's pretty easy to think about what you "could have" or "should have" done differently. Hindsight *is* 20/20 after all.

But what if I told you that the type of preparation you need to undertake for change is not in stockpiling supplies, creating escape plans, or stashing extra money away for a rainy day? What if I told you that the most important thing you can do to get ready for change—any kind of change—is in the way you *think* about change?

Your mind is powerful. You have the power to create new things and make them a reality by simply imagining what's possible. When you imagine what can be, you unleash the greatest force ever—the power of creation. By creating what's possible in your mind, you can lay the foundation for whatever new reality you desire.

But being prepared for change is more than just snapping your fingers and saying, "Think change." To truly lay a foundation that is conducive to embracing and managing the process of change, you must first accept and establish new baselines. These will guide you and prepare you to think, act, and be different before, during, *and* after change.

This begins by examining your foundation of perception and perspective. The decisions that you make are largely based on those two things. *Perception* is the way that you see things and process situations based on information that you acquire through your senses. *Perspective* is based on your attitude and the way you feel about something, in other words, your point of view. To put it simply, perception is shaped by your interaction with the world, and perspective is influenced by the way you feel about the world. To become equipped to manage and embrace change, you must be aware of both your perception and perspective and understand how they influence and inform your decision-making and actions.

My perception prior to Hurricane Katrina led me to conclude that the warning signs around me were no big deal. Things happened as they always did. Every time a storm rolled through, I would think about the issues (because they were right in front of me), but once the storms moved past and things calmed down, I forgot about any warnings or cause for concern. I became numb to the danger because I had been lulled into a false sense of security. I may have seen the same warning signs as other people, but because I *perceived* that those weren't real threats to me, I dismissed them.

My perspective as someone who was accustomed to living through mild hurricanes and coming out unscathed made me think that I was invincible and not at risk for a catastrophic storm. Being impacted by storms just wasn't something that happened to *me*. People who aren't "used to" certain situations tend to have a heightened sense of awareness or concern about them, but the more you go through the same cycles, the more you brush them off as something you don't have to worry about. It just doesn't happen to you, so no need to be concerned.

How many times has this happened to you? You've gotten so comfortable with things being a certain way that your brain tells you, "Nothing to see here," and you keep it moving. Doing this means that, many times, you end up overlooking something that's right in front of you that should have screamed WARNING!

Think for a moment about the global pandemic and how woefully unprepared organizations were for COVID-19.

The warnings that, in hindsight, were right in front of us the entire time were completely overlooked and ignored. Our perception of our own invincibility and belief that we could weather any storm—and are, in essence, untouchable—led to catastrophe. How many times had issues surrounding our health-care system been discussed? How many studies and reports had been issued on health and wealth disparities? How did we ignore the advanced warnings right in front of us as China and Europe dealt with the spread and devastation of the disease?

The same thing happens in a lot of teams and organizations where things have always been done a certain way. Because your systems and processes are familiar to you, you don't register the warning signs that are right in front of you. Your perception is that because things are "working" (not necessarily working well), there's no problem, no warning system to be aware of and consider. Therefore, the prevailing attitude is to keep it moving. There's nothing to see here. Therefore, you miss the opportunity to make adjustments and to prepare for chaos that could be lurking right around the corner.

When new people enter the equation, they don't have the same perception or perspective that you have. Their view hasn't been conditioned through a lens of familiarity to see warning signs as "normal." They don't accept the prevailing belief that everything is "fine." So they ask questions. They voice their concerns. And in many cases, they are advised to be silent, to adjust and accept what everyone else sees and does because "that's the way it's always been done."

So how do you "fix" this? How do you lay a new foundation and better prepare for change? Short answer—by being consciously aware of what is going on around you and within you. You cannot prepare for change if you don't even see that change is possible, probable, or inevitable. Preparing for change isn't a checklist of things to do or rules to follow. It's a recognition that you must be aware, willing to act, and open to doing things differently even if what has always been done has seemed to "work" in the past.

As an agent for change, you will sometimes be the lone voice. You will be told "no" more times than you can count. You may even be ostracized or passed over for opportunities because you refuse to "fit in." That's part of the job description. When you have the burning desire to shift things for the better, you won't rest until things start to move.

Preparing for change requires you to be open to change. To listen to that still, small voice that causes you to pause by quietly whispering that something is "off." It means you must be open to seeing things around you through a different lens. Your perception and perspective will need to be challenged instead of blindly accepted. Create opportunities for others to weigh in and offer their own assessment of the situation. As a change agent, you must be willing to be open to challenging your own way of thinking and inviting others to challenge them as well before you can ask someone else to do the same.

To effectively prepare for change, you must learn to ask certain questions that will enable you to think ahead. The goal is to frame situations in ways that help you see beyond your preconceived notions and dig deeper to see what's underneath.

Your questions should challenge you to see things differently and also provide you with a level of certainty that you are embarking on the right path. Some specific questions that come to mind include:

- What is the best that can happen?
- What is the worst that can happen?
- What do I know for certain about this situation?
- What questions remain unanswered?
- What is it about this situation that makes me feel safe and secure?
- What is it about this situation that gives me pause?
- Who are the best people to have with me in this situation?
- Who am I missing on my team?
- What strengths do I /my team have that we bring to this situation?
- What weaknesses do I/my team have that will impact this situation?
- What opportunities are there in what is to come?
- What threats are there in this situation?
- What resources are needed to handle this successfully?
- What does success look like?
- What outcomes do I want to see?
- What commitment is required to effectively manage this situation?
- What is it that I don't know?

The purpose of these questions is to push you beyond what you think you already know in order to help you to think more deeply and fully about the situation. You can't prepare for what's coming if you aren't willing to see the situation fully from several different angles and perspectives. That said, it is virtually impossible to plan for every single possible contingency or potential outcome, so don't obsess over this part of the process. The key is to be detailed and thorough but to avoid paralysis by analysis. You still have to act. You don't have the luxury of spending *all* of your time analyzing what might be coming. At some point, the analysis and preparation that you've done will have to suffice, and it will be time to move forward.

Once you have examined the situation from various angles and asked the right questions to expand your thinking and viewpoint, it's time to create a plan of action. This plan is what amounts to your blueprint or map that will guide you in what happens next. When you create a plan of action in this step, you are beginning the process of equipping your team and yourself to know what to do and when. This type of preparation must be done before you're in a change or crisis situation for the simple fact that you'll have a hard time planning while you're emotional or stressed. It's the same logic inherent in having an evacuation plan or conducting fire drills when things are fine. You want to run through the steps to make sure everyone knows what to do and when *before* things get crazy. Waiting to plan and practice your action steps in the midst of a change event or crisis is too late. At that point, you've missed the opportunity to plan and prepare, and now you're in full blown reaction mode.

Widespread sentiment was expressed after the fact that I (along with countless others) did not take Hurricane Katrina seriously enough. Fast and furious opinions, commentaries, and various op-eds flew from every direction—we should have evacuated; we endangered ourselves needlessly; we didn't listen to the experts; etc., etc., etc. What's not considered is that I (along with countless others) took the same actions that we had for previous storms. I had a standard hurricane preparedness kit and checked off a series of steps once it was confirmed that the city was indeed in the path of the storm. The windows were boarded up and taped to avoid flying glass. I had purchased bottled water and individual servings of canned fruit along with extra batteries for the flashlights and candles in case we lost power. I packed an overnight bag just in case I needed to leave suddenly, along with a number of other items on the checklist. These were my standard protocols, and the plan that I followed was based on my prior experience with hurricanes and the standard information shared by authorities, news outlets, and disaster-preparation agencies. Hindsight is always 20/20. It's easy to second-guess the steps that were taken *after* an event when you have the benefit of knowing exactly how things unfolded. Preparation before the event is a completely different animal.

I mention all of that to say this: don't beat yourself up trying to overprepare. When you do all that you can think to do and look at the situation from every possible angle, at some point you're just going to have to say, "Let's go," and just roll with it. You can't be expected to predict the future. No one has a crystal ball that allows them a full video of the change event in high definition for them to review and dissect in slow motion. At some point, you'll have to trust yourself, your team, and your plan and move on from there.

What will ultimately distinguish you from those who fail to plan and prepare at all is that 1) you will have asked yourself more in-depth, thought-provoking questions than most, and 2) your preparation won't stop with what happens before the event. When you adjust your thinking to consider various options, opportunities, and outcomes, you will naturally enter a mindset of constant analysis, observation, and inquiry. This shift in the way you think will extend beyond what happens before the event to how you respond during the event.

Preparation and adjustment should also occur in the midst of the change event. You can always prepare yourself for what's coming next, even when the clock has already started ticking and change is upon you. You just have to shift your mindset and reset your thinking to enable you to think calmly, rationally, and systematically. Whatever you believe about change and your process during change is what will be. If you want to start to change your results and outcomes during and as a result of change, then you have to begin with the way you think about change.

"Whatever you believe about change and your process during change is what will be."

CHAPTER 2

The Mindset of Change

I n my journey navigating all types of change events, I have
developed a few principles that have allowed me not only
to get through change but also to *succeed* through change.
These are the principles that I will share with you through
our journey together. They are the same principles I used
to create an approach that I have shared successfully with
teams, organizations, and leaders to facilitate outcomes,
create dynamic learning collaboratives, and create success.

Psst … pay attention. I'm going to let you in on a little
secret before we go any further. This statement, this one fact,
is the basis for all the other premises that I will share. If you
don't accept this one underlying premise, then everything
else that I'll share with you will mean nothing and, to be
honest, won't do you any good. You'll be left with just another
book that you read that didn't do much to make a true impact
on you, your team, or your organization.

What makes this process different from what you've
experienced in the past is that I want you to shift the
way you THINK about change. I'm not talking about the
multiple steps, approaches, and theories of change. I'm
not focusing on all of the organizational strategies that
can be implemented to deal with change. No. I'm focusing
specifically on the *people side of change*. And in this

approach, it is important to think about change through a personal lens. As such, you have to shift your perspective to know and accept this one underlying truth if you want to achieve success:

Change begins in the mind.

I already know what you're thinking: "Keisha, how can change *begin* in the mind when it's an event that happens in the world around me or something that happens *to* me? I don't think about an event, and then it happens. Something happens, and then I have to deal with it. Shouldn't we be focusing on that and talk about how to deal with different events if I want to be prepared?"

The short answer is, well, no. Remember: I told you earlier that change is a process that begins with an event. If you don't understand and accept the role of your mind in this equation and the way that you think about change, especially the way you think during the *process* of change, then you're doomed to repeat the same old cycles that have led to failure or less than desirable results. The reason you're reading this book is because you *don't* just want to do what's been done before. That hasn't worked, and no one willingly wants to remain stuck in the same old cycle of event, react, and repeat.

The way you think about the event and what leads up to the event has a huge impact on the process of change and your ultimate success or failure. To prepare yourself *for* the process, you first have to shift your thinking to be open *to* the process and then adjust your thinking *during* the process. That means you have to be open to thinking about change differently as a whole.

Remember that example I gave in the last chapter about perspective and perception? I found myself in my living room waiting on an approaching storm for one reason and one reason only—I hadn't allowed myself to think that there was a *possibility* that I could be sitting in a boarded-up house directly in the path of a Category 5 storm. All the other storms had passed us by or had been underwhelming. How in the world could I end up here?

Even with all the warning signs around me that this storm was different, I didn't "see" or accept them because in my *mind* they weren't relevant or even real probable threats to be considered. After all, we hadn't had a really bad storm in years. Every year we went through the motions to prepare "just in case," but no one actually believed that we would get hit with something this bad. Even though I ultimately had no control over the change event that ultimately occurred (the actual storm), I found myself in the midst of it only because I didn't prepare for the likelihood or possibility of it in actuality being that catastrophic. Not only that, but I didn't *allow* myself to *think* about how I would respond to it if/when it DID arrive. That one act cost me dearly—emotionally, mentally, physically, financially, in time, resources, and opportunity.

When you don't open your mind to the possibility of change, you don't allow yourself the opportunity to respond appropriately to the process of change.

If you never believe that something is possible, you don't take the time and effort to consider it, plan for it, and expect it. That said, it's also important to understand the *ways* we have to think about change. It's not just enough to be open to considering the possibility of change or to plan ways to respond once change occurs. You also have to think differently about the way change resonates with you, impacts you, and drives you. This isn't what's considered "normal," but that's okay. That's the beauty of change. It happens.

Get Comfortable Being Uncomfortable

A "comfort zone" is described as a place or situation where you feel safe or at ease and without stress. It's a level where you function on autopilot and where ability and determination are not being tested.

Staying in your comfort zone is counterproductive to growth. Growth only happens when you're uncomfortable. The events and processes of change create situations that pull you out of your comfort zone and force you to face new situations that challenge your thinking.

Being equipped for change involves getting you to think about how you think before, during, and after change.

When you are thinking about the way you're thinking (metacognition), then you are more apt to recognize areas where you need to adjust, adapt, learn, and grow to become better. For example, think back to when you were first learning how to do something new, like driving a car. When you first got into the car, you had to think through every step in the process: positioning the seat and mirrors, checking your surroundings, putting the car in gear, steering, applying the gas and brake with the right amount of pressure (herky-jerky starts and stops were all too common in the beginning), not to mention incorporating the changes you needed to make to respond to different situations around you.

Before the act or steps of driving became second nature (where you didn't have to consciously think about what you were doing), you had to pay close attention to what you were doing to operate the car *and* the circumstances that were unfolding around you in order to make real-time decisions about what to do next. In the beginning, it was all about remembering which was the gas pedal and which was the brake and taking your time to make a three-point turn or parallel park. After you'd adjusted your thinking to accept the nuances of how you needed to process information and respond to situations, it became easier for you to travel longer distances and be more relaxed.

Fast forward to today. Your thinking has shifted to focusing on the directions or navigating roadblocks or detours along your journey. Because you're now more advanced, experienced, and comfortable with the process, there are times when driving a familiar route that you get in the car and really don't pay too much attention to how you end up at your destination. (Wait, you don't do this? I know I'm not the only one!)

The same thing happens when you become too comfortable in your thinking. When your mind isn't open to accepting new ways of thinking, being, or doing, you find yourself being resistant to change. It's like your mind goes on strike and your brain puts out a sign that says "no vacancy" to new ideas or concepts.

That kind of thinking and mindset can be dangerous in teams and organizations. To be honest, that kind of thinking is dangerous on so many levels in life—period. I wouldn't have ended up in a boarded-up house in the path of a storm if I had been more open to thinking about what was possible or probable. Your company, organizations, or teams wouldn't have ended up dealing with a crisis if you'd been more open to thinking about what change might bring.

When things are easy and comfortable, most people get lulled into a false sense of security. When something comes along that challenges that sense of security, it's usually not pretty, especially if they're not prepared.

Think about what happens when you're dealing with something new or challenging. Do you get flustered? Annoyed? Irritated? How do you respond when your abilities are tested? When things aren't so "easy" for you? Do you focus more and slow down, or do you rush through in order to "get it over with"?

You don't learn new things when you are familiar or comfortable with a process or situation. You learn and grow when you try something new or unfamiliar and when you are stretched beyond what you already know (or think you know). Only then are you really paying attention to what's going on around you (and within you). Your senses are heightened; you take in more information; your mind is awake and buzzing as you process all of the possible outcomes and try to make a decision about what you should do next.

Discomfort—or really just being jolted out of your routine—is what kick-starts your learning process. Instead of fighting anything new or unsettling, look at those as opportunities to learn and grow. Open your mind to the possibilities of what can be instead of remaining closed off and holding onto what you already know.

Simply put, you have to become comfortable with (welcoming or accepting of) being uncomfortable if you want to navigate and embrace change.

The way your mind processes information in times of challenge and discomfort determines how effective and successful you'll be through the process of change. Your perception and perspective positions you for the journey ahead.

It's not about the things that go on around you; it's the way that you think and what happens within you that determine your success.

When you understand this, you can begin to exercise more influence and impact over the *process* of change and create opportunities to learn and grow *through* change. Shifting the way change begins in your mind sets you on the path to success.

CHAPTER 3

The Process of Change

Change is an action word. It is not a one-time event or something that happens to you. It is something that begins a process within you that allows you to grow, learn, and become a better version of yourself. When we look at change as something that happens to us, we miss the opportunity to take action, create, influence, impact, and arrive at a different way of doing, being, and thinking.

Change is something that occurs all the time, but we don't usually focus on the process that unfolds after the event. Instead we tend to focus on what we didn't like or figure out ways to avoid the change process that needs to happen in order for us to lean into our discomfort. Embracing discomfort allows us to ultimately get out of and move past the limitations of our comfort zones.

Change is an individual process that occurs in a collective setting. You cannot measure your individual progress by everyone else's progress. This fundamental fact flies in the face of traditional forms of organizational evaluation where the leader is evaluated based on the progress of the team. Yes, you want to evaluate the progress that everyone in your charge is making. But you cannot compare people's individual journeys or take credit for someone else's process and progress. Change requires you to do the internal work to be focused on your growth and your development. It encourages you to determine how you impact the world around you instead of allowing the world around you to impact you.

Change continues long after the feeling has passed, and the emotions have waned. It still goes on when attention has shifted to other things. Just because you don't think you see it, doesn't mean it's not happening.

Change happens in shifts. Shifts in attitudes. Shifts in thinking. Shifts in conversations. Shifts in engagement. Shifts in relationships. Shifts in connecting. Shifts in writing. Shifts in what we tolerate and shifts in what we stand up for. The shifts of change occur as a result of and in the midst of the disruption of change. This disruption is a process.

Change is a process that begins with an event. Just because the event has passed, doesn't mean we won't forever be transformed by the ripple effects of the process. The bigger the change event, the bigger the ripple effects and the longer they are felt.

Change requires a reckoning. You will have to face your shortcomings. You will have to admit your faults. You will need to step out of your comfort zone. You will have to be transparent and vulnerable and open to difficult conversations.

Anything less than a full reckoning is lip service. Platitudes don't support movement. Token gestures don't cultivate trust. Do or don't do—there is no try. Change is a process that begins with an event. Face the event. Embrace the process. Become the change.

Step 1: The Event (Catalyst)

My life—both personally and professionally—has been a masterclass in change. Success has come not as a result of being able to react to what some may call the "big" changes (large, sudden events). Instead, I have found success because of my capability to shift, adapt, and navigate through the process before, during, and after the event.

Everyone usually thinks of change as being defined as "something that happens." When you think about change in terms of events or occurrences, you miss the opportunities for true growth and development that happen through the process of learning and exploration *after* the event.

Your view of change colors your relationship with change. When you see change as formidable, unwelcome, and sudden unwanted events that happen "to" you, you react to change by pushing back from it.

No one wants to be uncomfortable. No one craves upheaval or uncertainty. Therefore, when you think of change, especially within your companies and organizations, you see only situations to be dealt with, mitigated, and in most cases, moved past as quickly as possible. The pain and negative emotions that you feel during change events cause you to describe and think of change as something "bad," unwanted, and unwelcome.

> The first trickle of water on the floor beneath the front door looks like something had spilled, and I absently wonder if one of the dogs had knocked over a water dish or maybe had an accident. As I notice the amount of water spreading from the door to the baseboards, I realize that it isn't a spill on the inside—water is quickly coming into the house from the outside.
>
> I leap up and peer through the small opening at the top of the boarded-up window, only to see water

all around, covering my porch and starting to push its way into the house. In a matter of moments, water sloshes around my ankles and rises up around my calves, soaking my tennis shoes, making my feet feel heavy, slowing my progress, and making it difficult to run from room to room. The attic is the only place of refuge from the rising tide, so I slosh back and forth grabbing my dogs, emergency duffle bag, bottled water, and canned fruit, depositing each in turn up inside the attic. By the time I haul myself up, the water is chest high and the power has gone out, snuffing out all noise and plunging us into darkness.

As I sit in the attic with my feet dangling through the opening over the room below, I can't tear my eyes away from the water rising rapidly beneath my feet. An onslaught of wailing gale force wind shakes the foundation of the house, lifting a corner of the roof ever so slightly so that I get a glimpse of the world outside. I instinctively wrap my arms around the nearest beam above my head and pull down with all of my might. Whispering a breathless mantra of "hold ... hold ... hold ... hold," I concentrate my gaze at the offending corner of the roof that had moments before threatened to dislodge, as if I could will it to withstand the forces lashing against it.

My mind frantically races through possible scenarios of how this ultimately would end—none of them good—as I unsuccessfully attempt to block out the screams of my neighbors being awakened by water rushing into their beds. One thought breaks through the noise and the chaos and sticks in my mind: is this it?

The situation described above was what I faced during Hurricane Katrina in 2005. In that moment, I had a decision to make: how would I respond to the change that was in front of me? But even more importantly than what I did in that moment was what I would learn from the experience and how I would use that new knowledge to create my future moving forward.

When most people encounter change events, so often they immediately go into fight-or-flight mode—determining whether they will stand up and defend themselves or run away and try to save themselves from the situation.

Not all of you will experience anything as physically endangering and catastrophic as a category 5 hurricane, but you all have your own version of change events that you have had to live through and navigate. The issue is not in the size or intensity of the event itself, but rather in how you are equipped for it, what you do through it, and how you are impacted as a result of it.

Change events are often sudden, challenging, frightening, and complex. Rarely do they only involve one single thing that can be dealt with swiftly and easily. Instead, you're faced with several situations all at once that leave you feeling overwhelmed and outmatched.

Focus on the Change in Front of You

In the experience I just described, I'm in the midst of a Category 5 hurricane. Several different issues are being thrown at me all at once. Things I have to think through and decide how to address. I can't allow myself to sink into panic or despair. I don't have the luxury of numbing myself to the reality of the circumstances in front of me because it's staring me right in the face. I can't sit back and allow someone else to take over, because that's not an option. There are others depending on me, and more importantly, *I'm* depending on me.

So what to do? How do you deal with a change so swift and so large that it overwhelms you? What do you do when there are so many decisions that have to be made that you literally can't think straight enough to separate them all, much less actually address any specific one?

The change event is upon you, staring you in the face. What now? The key in this moment is not to default to fight-or-flight but to take the time to think through the event as you see it and formulate a plan of how to respond—not react—to it.

How do you respond to the change event that is in front of you?

Responding to the change event that is in front of you requires focus. You quite simply have to focus on what's immediately in front of you and examine all aspects of it. You cannot address current change events by bringing in other factors from situations before or others that you think may arise. Focusing on what is in front of you requires you to examine the change event *as it is*—not as you think it is or want it to be.

Let's stop right here for a moment. Notice I said you have to examine the change event *as it is—not as you think it is or want it to be*. Why the distinction? Because the way our minds strive to create meaning and make decisions involve recall (making connections to the past) and imagination (creating new things for the future). It's important for you to ensure that you are not seeing things through a lens of recall or imagination when making decisions.

How many times have you been in a conversation (or maybe an argument) with someone and noticed that they've either embellished the details around what you've said or maybe connected it to a memory or experience that they've had that changes the direction of the conversation? This connection or embellishment shifts the purpose and meaning of what you were originally trying to share and changes the entire complexity of the conversation. These adaptations or embellishments happen naturally in everyday interactions when you're not stressed or being challenged. Imagine what happens when you're in the midst of a crisis? If you're not aware of how you're thinking during change events, it's easy to get derailed and upended by your own thoughts.

Focusing during a change event requires discipline. Change is emotional. Change is personal. Change is unsettling. Change is unnerving. There are so many different nuances that arise when faced with a change event that it sometimes makes it difficult to know what to do, much less actually take clear action.

Remember when I said change begins in the mind? Well, the way that you think about a change event determines whether you're going to get through it successfully or not. If you try to think about everything all at once, you're doomed. If you only focus on one small part of the change event and ignore everything else, you're still doomed.

Don't want to be doomed? Don't make things too complicated—but also don't oversimplify. You need a balance. It's important to break down large change events into manageable steps that will allow you to focus your attention and efforts on things that you can accomplish. Those manageable steps are things that you can focus on individually while still understanding and considering their connection to the overall issue or goal.

When faced with overwhelming or uncertain circumstances, give yourself permission to act quickly and decisively, but also equip yourself to be in position to act by preparing your mind to act. That requires you to adjust the way you think about change. Understand the need to focus on what's necessary for this particular point in time so that you can lay the foundation for future long-term success. Everything is connected. Nothing that happens in a change event stands on its own. You always have to consider the connection, ripple effects, and impact on the big picture.

Let me clarify something. Focusing only on what you need to do in this moment is what people naturally do when they're only looking at the event in front of them. In those instances, they're usually only trying to ride the wave to get to the other side. The difference between them and you is that they're not really committed to long-term change. What I'm asking you to do is to shift your thinking to consider what you need at this point in time, but as it relates to laying a solid foundation for future long-term success, not just to get through this moment. In other words, *your "right now" thinking needs to have a "what's next" filter*.

Take Action

To enhance your focus during a change event and maintain that focus during the change process, try these three steps:

1. Put first things first: identify what you're going to focus on (as specifically as possible).

2. Envision success: determine what outcome you want to see in action.

3. Plan the work and work the plan: determine what action *must* be taken and what *can* be taken in this moment.

Let's examine these in a bit more detail. *Put first things first. Identify what you're going to focus on as specifically as possible.* When several components of change events are swirling around you, it's important to narrow down the issues that you need to address. You can't address all of the issues facing you at once anyway, so do yourself a favor and start by breaking down the complex change event into all of the specific parts that need to be addressed. A word of caution: when you list out all of the different components and issues that need to addressed, don't fall into the trap of feeling more overwhelmed because you've now actually named everything that's staring you in the face.

The purpose of the naming/listing exercise is not to overwhelm you, but rather to help organize your thoughts and provide some guidance to help you *prioritize* what needs your attention. This is also a good way to analyze or assess the overall issues and determine what's broken or not working properly. Doing this also enables you to see how different components or areas of the change event may be interconnected. If something is connected to or impacts something else, then the actions you take can have a ripple effect that may address more than one issue at a time.

Once you have all the different issues listed, then identify what you're going to focus on and address first. Ask yourself: What's the main thing? What needs to be handled first? Be specific. The more vague you are, the more room for error and the more apt you are to engage in what is known as "scope creep." Scope creep happens when you start off doing one thing and end up gradually adding more small things so that in the end you've created a much larger issue than when you started.

Having a hard time picturing what I mean? Here's an example. You've spent the weekend logging some serious couch time, watching Netflix, and sustaining yourself on a steady diet of your favorite snacks. Because you're in "chill mode," you haven't moved during the past half day spent binge watching a series that you don't even know how you got roped into. You get a call from a friend telling you they're coming over, so you decide to tidy things up a bit.

You start by picking up the discarded wrappers, empty chip bags, and soda cans on the floor next to you, but then you realize that you can't possibly carry them all to the trash can. So you place them in a pile with the idea to go get the trash can and bring it to the pile. As you turn to go into the kitchen to pick up the trash can, you notice the couch cushions that have fallen on the floor.

As you begin straightening up the couch cushions, you discover the crumbs that have found their way beneath the cushions, and you realize it would probably be easier to use the vacuum than trying to pick them all up by hand. You go to the hall closet and pull out the vacuum and take care of the cushions, and then decide you should probably vacuum the carpet in the living room while you've got it plugged in. Once you finish the carpet in the living room, you decide to vacuum the hallway since you have to walk back that way to put away the vacuum cleaner.

On the way down the hall with the vacuum cleaner, you realize that you should probably vacuum the bedrooms too while you're there. When you walk past the hall bathroom on the way to the second bedroom, you realize that you should probably clean the bathroom since your friend might need to use it at some point during the evening, so you leave the vacuum in the doorway, walk into the bathroom, open the cabinets beneath the sink, and start pulling out the cleaning supplies.

As you start cleaning the bathroom, you realize you have to empty the trash. On the way to take the trash out you pass the living room and see the snack wrappers on the floor where you left them as you were cleaning the cushions. At this point you still have the snack wrappers on the floor, the vacuum cleaner is still out, the bathroom is half-cleaned, you haven't gotten dressed, and the living room still isn't clean.

Then the doorbell rings.

Sound familiar? Imagine how this would be compounded if you were stressed, in a state of heightened emotion, and in the midst of a major change event. Sure, getting distracted while tidying up your living room isn't nearly as important as being trapped in your attic during a Category 5 hurricane, but the tendencies you exhibit when you're relaxed are multiplied and amplified during moments of stress or anxiety.

Change is emotional. Change causes stress. Change impacts your physical senses and your ability to think and act. Because you understand this, you must create a system and series of short steps that will enable you to navigate the process of change without becoming overwhelmed by the events of change.

Envision success: determine what outcomes you want to see in action. After you've identified the specific aspects of the change event that need to be addressed and determined which items you're actually going to address, think about what outcome you want to see happen. This is where you get to think about what success actually looks like in action.

Your mind is amazing in that it has the ability to imagine and create. Ever had an experience where you didn't know all the details of what was going on, but your mind filled in the blanks and created a whole scenario that wasn't even true? (Think about a mother trying to call her child repeatedly late at night while the child is out, and her calls keep going to voicemail. Her imagination likely invents the worst-case scenario to explain why her child isn't answering.) That's the power of imagination! Well, instead of using that power to create visions of the future that may cause you fear or anxiety, use that ability to see (in your mind's eye) what success looks like in action.

To create a vision of success with the outcomes you want to see in action, you need to ask the right questions. What does this look like in real time? What does it feel like? What specifically am I doing? Who else is involved? What needs to be different in order for this to happen? Even if you don't know specifically what you *do* want success to look like, you know what you *don't* want, so at the very least, begin with the opposite of that.

The most important part of this process is to allow your mind to go beyond your current circumstances and create a picture of what you want to happen, instead of being limited by the current situation. Often when dealing with change events, it's easy for your attention to be pulled into focusing only on what's in front of you. Yes, that's an issue that needs to be addressed—and it will be—but only after you're able to see your way clear to how much better things will be on the other side.

If you can't see yourself actually doing something different, then it's more difficult to take the steps to make success happen. Your mind creates a type of self-fulfilling prophesy because it paints a picture of what things will look like in the future. Once this vision is in your head, you follow through with your actions to make it happen. Picturing what success looks like in action shifts your mind from focusing on the issues or problems causing you distress or anxiety to amplifying solutions that give you hope and direction. *What your mind focuses on, you get more of*—remember that.

Plan the work and work the plan: determine what action *must* be taken and then determine what actions *can* be taken in this moment. Those two things may not be the same. It's very important to differentiate between the two when crafting your action plan. When you plan the work and work the plan, you're being strategic, realistic, and intentional about where to spend your time, effort, and resources. If you don't take the time to map out what should be done, could be done and then identify when it will be done, then you run the risk of spinning your wheels and wasting both time and effort.

Once you've envisioned what success looks like, then you can create a plan to get there. I call this process Deconstruction:Reconstruction. This is where you unpack the pieces of the vision to create the action steps that will get you there. What is needed (specifically) to make that happen? Who do you need on your team? What actions need to take place? Who needs to be involved? How much time do you need to make this a reality? In what order do things need to happen? Use the answers to these questions to create a road map of what needs to be done, when it needs to be done and who needs to do it. Keep in mind that you don't have to do everything alone. Involve your team and others who can help.

Change is a disruptor. It shakes up the way you naturally think and act. Because of that, you can't be certain that you'll naturally know what to do and be able to prioritize things quickly "on the fly." Reacting is never a good strategy. Responding to a change event by crafting a plan and following the plan to create the desired result is a much better way to manage change and ensure success.

A Word of Caution

Don't fall into the trap of immediately wanting to abandon everything that you learn (throwing the proverbial baby out with the bath water) when faced with a change event. The natural human reaction is to get rid of or move away from what's causing pain or discomfort. Think about how many times you've started—and stopped—a new weight loss routine or thrown out that New Year's resolution to exercise more when it got uncomfortable or inconvenient.

> **When you are faced with a new way of thinking and doing things, it's natural to want to abandon the discomfort to go back to the things that you're used to.**

Instead of getting rid of things that don't fit into your comfort zones, why not take the opportunity to reexamine the circumstances, situation, and processes to see what works and what doesn't, determine the source of the disconnect, and make *informed* decisions about what you can actually do to address the event? This is necessary for two reasons: 1) you have to know what's broken or uncomfortable to know exactly where to focus your efforts; and 2) you need to know what to adjust and adapt, so you won't recreate the same issue later.

Effectively dealing with a change event requires a sense of purpose and dedication. You can't "fake it till you make it." Instead, you have to "learn it as you become it." There are no shortcuts in this process. You have to be strategic, intentional, and aware as you think through the steps that you take. Addressing issues that arise due to a change event must be a priority if you want to move the needle and create opportunities to make an impact and bring about long-lasting, sustainable success.

Embrace the Stillness

If you're honest, on most days there are more things than you care to think about pulling at you from every direction: family, finances, professional responsibilities, personal issues and goals, physical considerations, and mental needs, to name a few. You have decisions to make and steps to take, but because of forces beyond your control, you just can't seem to make a move. Honestly, you're just, well … TIRED.

Tired of moving constantly. Tired of thinking nonstop. Tired of always having to figure out what's next. But what about the now? What are you missing or overlooking in the now because you're so focused on what's next?

Change is a process that begins with an event, but it's so easy to focus on the event so much so that you miss the process. That's because a large part of that process happens in the stillness of doing nothing.

In the stillness, you can rest. Rest has become overrated and looked down upon in our "get it done now" and "team no sleep" culture. Rest is essential for healing, replenishing, and rejuvenation. You can't pour from an empty cup, so you have to take time to rest.

In the stillness, you can connect, not just with others but also with yourself. When you're in constant motion, you lose touch with yourself. The noise around you drowns out the voice within you, and you forget what you want, who you are, and who you are becoming.

In the stillness, you can reflect. Take the time to look at the past and the present to identify lessons learned and things that you missed in the act of doing. Reflection is a necessary part of the process of growth and change because it allows you to see things from a different perspective—away from and outside of your emotions.

In the stillness, you can craft a response, not a reaction. You want to constantly move and do because you are fearful and your fight-or-flight instincts kick in. But what if you took some time to step back ... breathe ... and get the information necessary to make informed decisions and respond effectively instead of reacting emotionally? How much better would your outcomes be? Remember that emotions are temporary, but informed decisions are necessary.

During the process of change, you have to build in time for the stillness: reflection, meditation, and mindfulness. You should learn to practice an awareness of what you're thinking. Be present in the moment and conscious of your thoughts, feelings, and emotions. Doing this will equip you to make better decisions and recharge your mind to navigate the process successfully. If you're anything like I used to be (okay, still am at some points—I'm a work in progress), you have a very hard time being still because you feel that you should be productive at all times. It's very easy to fall into the trap of constantly feeling that taking time to just be still is somehow time wasted.

But why wouldn't you feel that way? Society is always reinforcing the message that you must be constantly on the go. Social media is steadily feeding you images of people who seem to have it all together and are crushing it. They're writing books, launching new companies and programs, and living their best lives! So why aren't you?! These subconscious messages disrupt your natural process of change and make you more anxious instead of more aware. Don't run from it or try to hide from being still. Embrace the stillness.

Stillness builds strength. It promotes understanding, prepares you for what's next, and positions you to take better care of yourself so that you can be better for others. In the stillness is where you discover who you really are and prepare for who you want to become.

Try This: Take Fifteen

When I tell people about the power of embracing the stillness and how they need to take time to be still, the first response I get is "but I don't have TIME!" You don't need to *have* time; you need to *take* time. So here's a very easy way for you to integrate embracing the stillness into your day.

Start with fifteen minutes a day. It can be in the morning before you get up and moving, during your lunch break, before or after dinner, or before you go to bed. It doesn't matter when you do it, just choose a time when you will commit to taking your fifteen minutes to be still. During this time, you don't actually do anything. You're just quiet. This is a way for you to begin to retrain your mind to be still.

This is very important. During this time, you must be still. Don't listen to music or podcasts or audiobooks. Don't use the time to catch up on emails or text messages. Don't use the time to make a list of other things that you need to do later. Don't phone a friend. Don't fold laundry, do housework, organize your desk, or take out the trash. Just. Be. Still.

Set an alarm or timer for fifteen minutes and allow yourself to fall into the stillness. At first it might drive you bonkers, but eventually you'll get used to it, and the time will actually start to go by pretty quickly. After you have become comfortable with one fifteen-minute period, add another fifteen minutes at a different time of the day. After you have become comfortable with those two sessions, add a third session and then a fourth until you're spending a total of an hour a day in stillness.

It's important to schedule these sessions during four different time periods of the day—in the morning, midday, early evening, and at night before bed. Doing this exercise will accomplish two goals: 1) it will teach you how to become comfortable with being uncomfortable; and 2) it will provide you with some much-needed quiet time in order for you to reset and center yourself throughout the day.

Learning to stop and be still before pivotal decisions when you may be emotional or feeling overwhelmed is a great way of equipping yourself to make better decisions and navigate change in more productive ways. It is also a great way to spend time getting to know yourself.

Step 2: The Shift (Transformation)

Who Are You in a Crisis?

Most people fear not being "enough." No one wants to feel inadequate. You don't want to feel out of control or "less than" or shame. Admitting to not knowing or even saying "I don't know" is not usually an acceptable response to a problem or crisis. People want answers, so not knowing brings up feelings of inadequacy or impostor syndrome where you doubt your accomplishments or ability and have a persistent, internalized fear of being exposed as a fraud.

To combat these feelings, you create alter egos or different "faces" that you show the world. Beyoncé famously admitted that she created a stage alter ego called "Sasha Fierce" when she had to perform because she was so shy. My alter ego "KiKi" shows up whenever I need a bit more toughness and a no-nonsense attitude. Whether you create an official alter ego or simply switch to your "Olivia Pope" mode to "handle it," the bottom line is that whomever you show to the world is still YOU—just the "better" version that you feel fits the situation or is better equipped to take care of things.

There's nothing wrong with having a different aspect or part of your personality to call upon as your go-to or as a boost or pick-me-up for your confidence. A problem only arises if you go to your alter ego so often that you start to lose your true self in the process.

Being comfortable in your own skin and the changes that you go through as you grow, learn, and develop is important for success. Crisis and unexpected change highlight who you really are at your core. The dominant parts of who you are show up under stress when you're in flight-or-fight mode.

> I lose track of time as the storm rages outside. There is no electricity, no window to see outside, no way for me to tell how long I've been holding onto the beam above and pulling down with all of my weight. I slowly realize that my arms are tired and sore, which is a sure sign that I've been in this position for quite some time.
>
> The screams from my neighbors quieted long ago, and now there's just an eerie silence. There had been another period of stillness earlier that seemed out of place. One minute the house was shaking from the

impact of the elements outside, the wind sounding like a freight train as it swirled relentlessly around me; and then all of sudden, there was dead silence. It seemed that everything in the world had just stopped, almost as if someone had hit pause in the movie of my life to go grab some popcorn. The silence lasted for several minutes, and when the wind began raging again, I figured out that the eye of the storm had passed over, so that must mean the end was near.

As I brace for the back side of the hurricane, I start to think about what might be next. From everything I had heard on the news, Hurricane Katrina has the highest wind speeds and greatest amount of torrential rainfall on the back end, so she is definitely going to pack a punch on her way out. I adjust my grip on the beam above me, check the level of the water beneath my feet (which thankfully stopped rising after reaching four rungs on the ladder below the attic opening), and take a few deep centering breaths—slowly in, hold, then slowly out.

In that moment, it dawns on me. I am no longer afraid. I don't allow my mind to wander and fill in the gaps of what I don't know with wild images of devastation fueled by my panicked imagination. I refuse to wonder about what has happened to the people I no longer hear screaming. I don't think about "what if" anymore. I don't question why. My only focus is to hold on, listen intently, and plan for what lay ahead.

Change brings opportunities for transformation. I want you to think about this for a moment. Who are you *really*? In the midst of change, what version of you stands up?

More importantly, how do you adapt to change in ways that make you better? As you move from the catalyzing change event to the shift of transformation, it's important to know and understand who you really are, which determines not only how you show up but also how you lead and engage with others.

Be aware of yourself, your triggers, your trauma, your tendencies, and your reactions to situations and people. Observe, reflect, and document your thoughts and feelings as close as possible to the moment whenever possible. Journaling is a great tool to use in gathering your thoughts and reflections while also giving you a record of how things unfolded for later reflection and review.

Be honest with your feelings and emotions and understand how they impact others. The key to transformation is to understand what works, what doesn't, and then make decisions about how to adjust and adapt. Old habits can shift into new practices when you are aware of your tendencies and make a consistent effort to adjust your behavior.

Be open to adjusting, learning, and growing. No one is perfect, and people are allowed the grace and space to change. Try new solutions and options to see what fits. The key is to always align the truth with the journey of transformation that you are traveling. You can't fool yourself into thinking that you are farther along than you are or that you are something that you're not. Be patient with yourself and love yourself enough to trust the process.

Knowing yourself is key to understanding who you are in relation to others. The way you engage or interact with other people during change, crisis, or stressful situations brings into play a different dynamic. In order to create opportunities for success, you have to be aware of all the different dynamics at play and adjust accordingly.

The Teachable Moment of Transformation

Change is a constant. Things in life are always shifting, growing, and evolving. Transformation is what happens when you turn the corner and the light comes on—that "ah-ha" moment when you now **know** better, so you can do better without too much thought. It's that moment when you go from having to think through every action when driving a car to operating almost on autopilot so that you can adjust to situations in real time without a lot of effort.

Transformation results in a permanently altered state. You don't have to think about not going back to the way you were, behaving or thinking like you did in the past. You just don't do it because you're not "that" person anymore. Most times you can't predict when that shift—that moment when you cross to the other side—will actually occur. One minute you're the "old you," and it seems like in another instant, you're *different*.

The truth is, during the process of change, you start with a catalyst event, then move into a "shift." This shift is where the transformation occurs. It's where the teaching and learning happens that changes who you are and how you think. If you are open to it and receptive during it, the shift is where you will unlock the gifts, talents, and abilities that have been lying dormant, waiting for you to unleash them. The shift is where you dig deep. It is the time when you face the uncomfortable reality of your limitations, both real and imagined. The shift is where you arrive at the crossroads of decision. The place where you have to decide if you are going to go back from whence you came, stay where you are, or move forward into the new and unknown. This decision-making process is what matters most. This moment, this instant, this is the teachable moment in transformation.

I wait and strain my ears to listen more intently. There is no mistaking it. It is quiet. No wind. No rain. No screams. Nothing. Just ... stillness. As I hold my breath, waiting for some clue, some movement, some sound that would give me an idea of what lay beyond the walls of my attic, I have a decision to make. Should I go out into the unknown or wait here to be rescued?

In my moments of indecision, the stillness is just as deafening as the storm had been over the course of the previous hours that I thought would never end. This silence, this pause, this place of being "in between" was a moment that I had pushed through and shaken off before in other situations. But today for some reason, it feels more ... real ... more important.

After a few moments of internal debate, I decide that I can't stay inside this sweltering attic much longer. The heat is becoming unbearable. And since there is obviously no way to escape by venturing below into the fifteen feet of water that fills my house, there is only one way to go, and I have to figure out a way to make it work.

The only tool I have at my disposal is a hammer. So I find a spot in the wall at the rear of the house and begin chipping and hammering away. My goal is to hopefully chip a hole big enough for me to crawl through and come out close to where I believe the lower roof of the drop-floor addition at the back of the house is connected. If I can get out there, I can stand on the lower roof and at least signal for help. At least, that's the plan.

Positioning myself cross-legged in front of the spot in the wall, I chip away at a small section of the pressed particle board. My focus and concentration are on that one spot. I don't look around at how small the attic is. I don't focus on my dogs and cat panting in the heat. I refuse to focus on the lack of ventilation or the cramped space that makes it impossible to stand upright. I focus all my attention and my energy on that one spot on the wall where my hammer strikes repeatedly.

I alternate between chipping with the sharp edge and pounding as hard as I can to break through. I curse the builders every time it looks like I'm going to gain access to the outside and instead encounter another layer of building material. Pressed particle board gives way to plywood and then a metal sheet (seriously??!!), which leads to more particle board, plywood, and finally, after countless hours, I can see a small pinhole of sunlight.

The glimpse of sunlight rejuvenates me, and I focus even more intently on my task. I don't have time for tears. I can't allow myself to succumb to the fear. I can't be paralyzed by the thoughts of what I might find once I do venture outside. I can't allow myself to entertain the possibility that I won't get out. I can't think about the very real probability of getting to the outside, only to find that I am all alone or that maybe, possibly, I won't be found at all.

People in the midst of the change process, react, and respond differently. Each person is operating at different levels based on their individual journeys. It's important to understand and be honest about where you are in your own journey so that you can engage with others accordingly. Some people face change and transition with steely resolve; others break down emotionally. Some people are quiet and introspective; others need action and conversation to feel like there's movement or progress.

So often when going through a change event as a team, group, or organization, it's easy for people to think of things based solely on their own perceptions and perspectives. Your reality does not automatically represent that of other people's journeys or places in their own process of transformation. People as a whole have a tendency to pass judgment on the actions of others based on the lens of their own experiences or thought processes.

When sharing aspects of my experience during Hurricane Katrina with others, it's common to hear people say what they "would have done" and either directly or indirectly berate me or infer that I was making "an irresponsible decision" by staying. Everyone has their own opinion; everyone thinks they know what they'll do or what's the best thing to do in the midst of their own change. However, it's important to remember that at the end of the day, we're all individuals. We each have our own thoughts, emotions, and tendencies. *Just because we're all in the same storm, doesn't mean we're in the same boat.*

Change provides an opportunity to learn by connecting the dots, talking to others, and using the new information to assist in building upon what you already know. The key is not to pass judgment on others because of our differences but to use the opportunity to learn from others in an effort to become better versions of ourselves.

Change Is NOT One Size Fits All

As human beings, we naturally want to compare our journeys, progress, and outcomes to others. Contrary to popular belief, comparison doesn't motivate you or give you any extra advantage. When you compare your journey to others, it's more often because you want direction and validation. Seeking confirmation of your direction, progress, and achievement by looking to or comparing yourself with others usually doesn't end well.

Best practices on the other hand, are examples of what has worked before in places or situations that are similar to yours. You use best practices when you don't want to reinvent the wheel; you want to jump-start the process; you need some guidance of what to do; and you want proof of success from someone who has gone before you. Think of it as living or learning vicariously through the benefit of someone else's lessons and experiences. Best practices provide *proven* examples of things that have worked before. They are only implemented based on careful analysis of the situation to ensure that the practices you're considering adopting actually align with what you're facing and where you want to go.

The key is to recognize that nothing is the same or constant about change because there are so many variables between situations and people. You have to learn to adjust and adapt even as you learn from the example of others, adopt new principles, and create relevant guidelines. As you navigate the process of change, it's important to account for variances and variables (i.e., people, processes, conditions, etc.). You will also need to identify what works and discard what doesn't based on *your* particular situation.

Being open to doing things differently is a cornerstone to managing change and embracing the transformational power of change. "That's the way we've always done it" is a death sentence for progress and innovation. Comfort zones are designed to maintain the status quo and keep you stagnant, not create new avenues for growth. Diversity of thought, experience, and implementation bring the best ideas to light and set you up for success.

Success looks different for everyone, so you need to identify the vision clearly and plainly. The process can have some detours, twists, and turns, so check periodically to make sure that you're still headed in the right direction. Recognize and celebrate the small victories to keep you motivated and remember that accountability, collaboration, and mentorship are key.

Overcoming Change Fatigue

As you focus on navigating the journey of change, I want you to keep in mind that change is a marathon, not a sprint. Most people are not exceptionally patient to begin with, and once you add in the uncertainty and discomfort that usually accompanies major change events, their patience level decreases tremendously. *No matter how much you want to, you just can't rush change.*

If you've ever gone on a long road trip with kids (or actually in some cases, adults), inevitably at some point someone will ask, "Are we there yet?" Change fatigue is when you get so tired of the discomfort in the process and impatient with the progress that you look around and ask, "Are we there yet?"

Maybe you're not seeing movement. Maybe the things that you *are* seeing aren't very encouraging. Maybe you're tired of talking about it, thinking about it, and having to deal with it. Maybe you're getting sick and tired of being uncomfortable and having to sit in your discomfort while you try to learn a new way and better way of thinking, being, and doing. Whatever the reason, you must learn to recognize change fatigue and implement strategies like the ones below to help you get through it.

Take a break. When you find yourself feeling frustrated, overwhelmed, or overcome by the process of change and dealing with all the nuances that entails, step back and take a break. Your brain needs time to process and absorb things. This whole "team no sleep" movement that seems to have taken social media by storm does nothing but cause unnecessary stress. If you want to be efficient and, more importantly, effective, you actually have to walk away for a bit to regroup. When you force yourself to keep pushing through even when you can feel your eyes glazing over, your temper growing short and your emotions running high, you're not being a good steward of your time and energy. More importantly, you're not taking care of YOU during the process of change.

Transformation requires A LOT of energy. It requires focus, reflection, adjustment, commitment, and dedication. You have to know and understand what you're doing and why you're doing it and be able to assess how you're performing all at the same time. That kind of mental energy requires frequent recharging. The "Take Fifteen" exercise makes a bit more sense now, doesn't it?

Do something different. I know, I know. I just said you need to take a break when you're feeling the effects of change fatigue. So how come I'm coming right back and telling you to "do" something instead? Hold on a minute and hear me out. Doing something different is actually another way of taking a break. The purpose of both strategies is to allow your mind to reset by shifting gears to something different from what you've been focusing on. When you walk away completely, you allow your mind to move away from thinking about the problem or issue at hand.

When you elect to do something different, you maintain a sense of activity but shake up your thinking process by having your mind engaged in something else. Shifting your focus activates different parts of your brain, and in some cases, if you choose something else that doesn't require a lot of deep thought, it might just be the thing to keep you occupied enough to allow your subconscious mind to work on the issue behind the scenes. Have you ever been doing some mindless activity and then all of a sudden—BANG—you get the ah-ha moment that cracks the code, the solution you'd been wrestling suddenly staring you in the face, clear as day? That's what happens when you do something different. It resets your thinking without completely shutting down your activity.

Check your progress. There are times when you feel as if you're not making any progress at all. Times when it seems like you've been in the wilderness of change *for-ev-er* and you honestly can't see an end in sight. Doing a progress check is where you take a look at where you started and then compare that to where you are today. If you've outlined a plan and have been following it (hint, hint—you should be based on my advice in step 1) and documenting your progress along the way, then checking your progress will give you a sense of accomplishment and pride of just how far you've come.

When you're battling through a particularly difficult time, it's so easy to feel as if you're spinning your wheels and thinking that you'll never reach your ultimate goal or destination. Periodic progress checks not only help to keep you motivated but also ensure that you haven't veered off path and are still heading toward the same goal. Or in some cases, they let you know that you may need to shift the plan a bit to better align with your goals. The bottom line is that there's nothing wrong with making adjustments. Just be sure that your adjustments are in alignment with keeping you on the path to achieve your ultimate vision.

Overall, making the shift during the period of transformation requires you to be intentional, not emotional; strategic, not haphazard; and consistent, not unstable. The process of getting to your "ah-ha moment" of making the shift isn't the same for everyone, so you'll need to be aware of and in touch with yourself to recognize when it happens. One thing to take note of—when you've come out on the other side of transformation, there is no going back to the way you used to be or the things you used to do. That's because transformation is the deepest, most profound and long-lasting part of change. It literally changes the composition of who you are at your core. It's not that you don't want to go back or choose not to go back—it's that you *can't* go back because that's just not who you are anymore.

In order to break the roller-coaster ride that usually accompanies change events and the wave of emotions and reactions that follow, a shift and true transformation must occur. During the global pandemic of COVID-19 and widespread protests against systemic racism that rocked the world, the prevailing sentiment among people was that this time was *different*. This time, there had been a shift in the way that we saw the world and our place in it. There was a shift in how we viewed our experiences and what we saw as important and worth speaking out about and fighting for. Only time will tell if the shift that we all felt was indeed real and if true transformation had taken place and we were finally ready for the final step in the process—the next normal.

Step 3: The Next Normal (Application)

Prepare for Your "Next" Normal

People want to "go back" to the way things were when faced with a change event because, by and large, they're creatures of habit and desire comfort. But once you have traveled through the process of change and experienced true transformation, you can't go back because both you and the circumstances you're facing are fundamentally different. It's like you're traveling the same road at different times of the day and during different seasons. The route may be similar, but the situations that you face each time (traffic, weather, detours, etc.) are different. So instead of spending time and energy trying to go back, why not seize the opportunity to create something new that now becomes your "next"?

Why do I refer to this as the "next" normal instead of the "new" normal? Well, simply put, change is a constant in life. Every time you encounter a new catalyst event and go through the shift of transformation, you arrive at what is now your next normal, or the next level in the process. The cycle constantly repeats itself. What is now your "next" stays that way until another event and you go through another cycle to arrive at your next destination. Thinking of your application stage as your "next" will prepare you to be flexible and anticipate the waves of the cycle.

Merriam-Webster.com Dictionary defines "normal" as "conforming to a type, standard, or regular pattern: characterized by that which is considered usual, typical, or routine" (as of October 11, 2020). Who sets the standard?

Who decides what's typical? Who determines what's expected? YOU! Now is the time to take advantage of the opportunity to create your next normal. The great thing about applying the lessons learned during the shift of transformation is that you get to determine what you want the next set of outcomes to look like.

What do you want to see? How do you want to be better? What new relationships do you want to form? What unexpected benefits and gifts have you discovered?

> After hours of chipping away at the wall in the attic, I finally make a hole big enough to squeeze through and survey the area around me. Standing on the roof of the addition to the house, I can see for the first time the devastation that surrounds me. Everywhere I turn, there is water. Power lines are down and lay dangerously against houses and other structures. Cars are submerged completely or in some cases have been transported from their driveways by the rising water and strong winds and come to rest perched on end and leaning against the side of houses. Boats rest on top of buildings in precarious positions, and all around me is an eerie silence.
>
> My eyes brim with tears, and I am filled with so many emotions all at once—relief at being alive, sorrow at the devastation around me, fear at the uncertainty of what lies ahead, and despair at the sheer weight of the complexity of the journey ahead of me. I have lost everything. My house, my car, my belongings—everything is gone. All destroyed in one night. There was no time to prepare myself for a loss of that magnitude. No time to adjust. No time to plan

for contingencies. I shake off my thoughts and turn my attention to the immediate task of figuring out what's next.

It's obvious that life as I know it is over. There is no choice of "going back" to the way things used to be. My house is filled with water, my car is flooded, my neighborhood looks like a war zone, and at this moment all I have is a duffle bag with one change of clothes and the shorts, tank top, and tennis shoes that I'm wearing.

Tragedy or opportunity? So often when faced with a change event, people focus so much on what they've "lost" that they miss the opportunity in front of them. Going through the process of transforming and shifting the way you think about situations and the world around you is key to being able to handle what's next and create your own opportunities.

When I emerged from my flooded house, all I could see in front of me was the destruction of life as I knew it. Everywhere I turned, there was proof that things would never be the same again and that I had to make a decision about what I wanted my new life to be. Picture it. In this instant, you have the opportunity to literally reinvent yourself. Everything that you knew is gone, and your life at this moment is a blank slate. What would you do? What would be your first thoughts? How would you determine what you wanted your next normal to be?

Every time you encounter a change event and go through the process, you have the same opportunity to create something new. Change is a pathway to reinvention if navigated properly. Instead of seeing change as losing something old, why not view it as creating something new as your "next"?

Pick a Struggle

I was having a conversation with a friend of mine about the process of writing this book, and I was sharing my frustrations (venting really) about all of the things that were going "wrong"—writer's block, an impending publishing deadline, and second-guessing how much of my personal journey and experiences to share. (Ironic, right?) I was pretty much overthinking the process of how to organize things and running down the list of so many other things that I had to do—blah, blah, blah. In the midst of this rant, she said one thing that stopped me mid-sentence: "Pick a struggle."

I was so taken aback that I just closed my mouth mid-sentence. Then I thought about it. How many times do you feel overwhelmed and outmatched because you fail to just pick a struggle? You can't do everything at once, but if you're like most people, you're certainly going to try—or at least worry about trying or not trying. When I emerged out of my attic onto the roof, I had so many things staring me in the face that needed to be dealt with. So many decisions to make that just thinking about it all could have paralyzed me.

When you're faced with the opportunity of creating a next normal, you can't allow yourself to get weighed down by thoughts of every single thing that needs to be done or addressed all at once. Pick a struggle. In other words, focus and finish. Envision what you want your next normal to look like, and then develop a plan and an approach to making that vision a reality. The key to creating your next normal is to embrace the opportunity before you. The process and journey of change that you went through was designed to equip and prepare you for your "next." It's up to you to decide what that next is going to be. Leave behind what no longer serves you and embrace the next things that come your way.

It's Okay to be Human

When change happens and things don't go the way you would like or hope, if you're anything like me, you've been told to be tough or strong. Having to make decisions comes with so many responsibilities and pressure that at times you may forget to be human and humane to yourself and others. Change brings its own set of intense feelings and emotions—confusion, anxiety, uncertainty, fear, stress, loss, and even grief over what used to be. Don't sweep these feelings under the rug or ignore them. More importantly, don't allow yourself to become overwhelmed or consumed by them either.

Learn to practice self-care. In creating and adjusting to your next normal, you'll need to be gentle and supportive with yourself. Even when you've arrived on the other side of transformation. Adjusting to thinking and being different takes time and patience. Identify your feelings. Name them, describe them, sit with them, and embrace them. Your feelings are nothing to fear. They show you things about yourself that you need to discover and learn from in order to grow.

Explore your feelings. Don't just wallow or be caught up or controlled by them. Dig deeper and ask yourself: what's causing you to feel the way you do? What events or triggers led up to your feeling this way? Examine your actions and emotions to learn where they come from, what they say about you and how to manage them.

Learn to release in healthy ways. Feeling overwhelmed by thoughts, decisions, or your feelings? Feel them, express them, and release them. Keeping things bottled up inside only causes more stress and anxiety. Dealing with the process of creating a new way of not only thinking and being but also showing up in the world and navigating new situations can be a bit much. Cry, laugh, dance, or be still—do whatever you need to do in the moment. Allow the feelings to flow through you and release them in positive ways that provide relief. Just don't put you or anyone else at risk or in harm's way.

Throughout your process of creating and adjusting to your next normal, be sure to take time or make time to reflect. Think about what's worked for you and determine what support you need to continue your journey. Identify ways you've healed and grown. Take an honest look at how things are progressing and identify what you want to do differently as you think about what's next. Becoming equipped for change goes beyond a series of steps and skills to enhance and improve your life professionally. It also includes self-care and taking the time to support your growth personally.

Learn to R.E.S.T.

Big changes don't come easily. The process of change, transformation, and adoption of a new way of thinking, being, and doing takes time, commitment, and consistent effort. Just because you've come out on the other side doesn't mean the journey is over. On the contrary, change is the only constant in life because the process is circuitous. Every time you think you've arrived, here comes a new catalyst, new shift, new transformation, and the next normal to adjust to and navigate. If you think about it, the cycle of change really should be called the Circle of Life.

To be honest, navigating this process over and over again can be exhausting if you're not properly equipped to handle it. That said, if you have the right tools and strategies in your arsenal, the process becomes easier to manage and you can become quite adept and successfully navigate it with ease.

Reflect. I've mentioned reflection a few other times so far, so that should give you an indication that this is an important skill to have. Reflection serves a different purpose depending on where you are in your development and what outcomes or next steps you're planning to take. At this stage in the process, you should reflect upon your challenges and successes and identify lessons that you've learned in your journey. Above all, you need to remember three things when it comes to self-reflection:

- *Be honest.* Rose-colored glasses prevent you from seeing the truth, so it's better to face situations clearly than to cloud the issue by hiding from your truth.
- *Be kind.* There's no need to be overly harsh or critical. You're human and allowed to make mistakes. That's how you learn.
- *Be thorough.* Cliff notes don't help you. Be detailed enough to include information that tells the whole story. Details about circumstances, choices, decisions, situations, and factors are important to the process.

Engage. You cannot make progress or changes unless you are fully engaged in the process. This isn't something that you can pay lip service to and expect long-term successful results. There are times when people show up for what I call the photo op of change. That's when they only want to be seen when the emotion and outrage are high, so they can be perceived as doing the work and committed to the process. It's not about who shows up in the moment and broadcasts to the world about their involvement. Navigating the process to facilitate real change requires the type of slow, consistent, behind-the-scenes connection and engagement to the process that attention seekers typically don't want. The key is to ask how you can engage in ways that are meaningful.

- *No half-stepping.* Show up. Be all in and ready to rock and roll. This means bringing your whole self to the situation every single time. This process requires your full attention and means that you need to be prepared to give your all. Doing any less than your best will not only negatively impact those who are depending on you but also ultimately derail your process of growth and hurt your development.

- *Be committed.* Commit fully to the process, no matter how uncomfortable it becomes. As I've said earlier, you must become comfortable with the discomfort if you want to be effective and successful in navigating change. Creating new systems and ways of thinking, being, and doing are not easy processes. You will have to become used to doing things that don't seem completely easy or natural while you adjust to the next normal that you're creating.

- *Be vocal.* Speak your truth—to others *and* to yourself. Own your process and journey of growth. Share your experiences and thoughts. Speak up and advocate for yourself and those who are experiencing the process and need support, guidance, and insight. Words have power. Use them.

   Strategize. Reacting never gets you anywhere of significance or anything of substance. Long-term change requires a strategic response. You have to think about your long-term goals, interests, and overall outcomes and then craft an approach and actions as a means to achieve them. Emotional reactions out of fear, pressure, stress, or triggers won't allow you to lay the proper foundation to achieve your goals and facilitate the outcomes that you envision and desire. In order to own the process, you have to make certain practices a part of your everyday tool kit:

- *Think it through.* When I spent eighteen months as a handyman's assistant doing odd construction jobs, I learned how to build a deck, repair a roof, install laminate flooring, install drywall, paint, renovate kitchens and bathrooms, and completed a host of other jobs that make me pretty handy around the house. One of the most important lessons that I learned from my boss was to look at things from all angles. Even if we had done a particular type of job multiple times before, we still needed to create a specific work plan for the job in front of us. We spent a significant amount of time up front thinking about the job from various perspectives and considering the impact different variables would have on our work process and the outcome we wanted to achieve. Only *after* we had devoted the time in the beginning to thinking and planning, did we start actually doing the work. An old construction adage I learned certainly applies here—measure twice, cut once. Or as I like to put it—*think twice, act once.*

- *Flesh out the details.* Once you have a strategy in place and have determined your approach, do the deep work of fleshing out the details in planning your course of action. Every little bit counts. Having grand plans is great, but success happens in the details. Take that strategic plan and drill it down to the specifics—what is needed to make that happen?

- *Question, question, and question again.* Inquiry is the best teacher. It allows us to do a deep dive into the causes, effects, and long-term impacts of our actions and the process. Ask yourself a series of questions to help you unpack what to do. What is the best that can happen?

What's the worst that can happen? What do I *want* to happen? What is needed to make this happen? The art of questioning allows you to tap into new ways of thinking, being, and doing.

Trust. Love yourself enough to trust the process. Uncertainty is expected when doing something new. The best way out of something difficult is to go through it. Forward movement builds momentum. If you trust the process and trust yourself as you navigate the process, then you'll be able to silence the doubt. Instead of allowing doubt to derail you, use it as a tool to highlight areas where you may be weak and need additional opportunities for learning, growth, and development. Once you've unpacked the uncertainty and learned all you can to create a solid plan of action, ditch the doubt and focus on execution.

By this point in the process you're trying to settle in and create a new rhythm and flow to the way life will be moving forward—or at least for the foreseeable future. There's still uncertainty, but you're adapting and will find yourself more seamlessly going through the steps in the process to do what's necessary in the moment. You can only do what you can do, so be gentle with yourself. Implement the steps outlined above to equip yourself to allay your fears, adapt, adjust, and move confidently forward toward success.

~~~~~~~~~~~~~~~~~~~~~~~~~~~

"Love yourself enough
to trust the process."

~~~~~~~~~~~~~~~~~~~~~~~~~~~

CHAPTER 4

From Triage to Trust

Reacting to change requires you to act instinctively and make quick decisions. When in reaction mode, your growth is not as important to you as your focus on results. The here and now is what matters most. This way of thinking narrows your perspective and creates tunnel vision because all you can see are the immediate circumstances you have to deal with. In this mode, you believe it's more important for you to be able to adjust on the fly than to move intentionally through the process. When you're in reaction mode your focus is on *survival*. That's triage—doing what you have to do in the moment.

In triage, you assign levels of priority to tasks to determine the most effective ways and order in which to deal with them. When you triage situations, there are essentially four categories to determine the level of urgency and priority of situations:

- *Immediate interventions*. These are urgent and need to be dealt with now. Think lifesaving interventions that can't wait.
- *Significant interventions that can be delayed*. These are serious situations that will need your attention but can wait a bit until you have more information, resources, and/or time.

- *Little or no intervention.* These are things that you can't really do much with in order to make a major impact or change in the situation.
- *Prepare for the loss.* These situations are so far gone that there's absolutely nothing you can do but prepare for the worst-case scenario and decide where to go from there.

Trust, on the other hand, allows you to plan. It expands your vision and focus beyond the here and now to consider what's next. *While triage is reacting to the first instinct, trust is planning the journey.* Trust requires a shift in the way that you think about situations in order to respond (not react) to them differently. Trust demonstrates a firm belief in the reliability of the truth, your ability, or strength. Trust is a foundation that you can use to build a solid plan of sound action.

As you navigate the journey of change, you develop the ability to move from handling situations as something to be triaged to learning to trust. Once you have crossed over into the realm of trust, you have become more comfortable with the process and are able to feel more in control, or at least feel more prepared to handle whatever comes your way. Navigating your next normal becomes second nature, and you find yourself able to breathe through the process, embrace the journey, and enjoy the experience. Trust creates confidence. The more comfortable you are in the process, the more confident you are and the more success you'll experience.

There's something to be said for developing a routine. Even though I am essentially living in my attic surrounded by devastation, I have managed to create some type of "normalcy." Other people have started making their way out of their flooded houses, gathering on the rooftops around the neighborhood. We would yell back and forth to each other asking questions at first, but since the sky became choked with helicopters yesterday, it's futile to try since we can't hear each other.

My days all seem to be more of the same, so they blend into each other for the most part. I take short naps instead of sleeping long hours and split my time between being outside on the roof—where, to shield myself from the blazing sun, I've erected a makeshift tent out of blankets and quilts stored in the attic—and taking refuge inside the sweltering attic. I've been rationing my one gallon of drinking water and several cans of fruit cocktail that I managed to reclaim from the refrigerator that floated past the attic ladder from the flooded kitchen below. There seems to be nothing to do but wait. On what, I don't know. There haven't been any attempts to rescue any of us as of yet. Just the endless buzzing of news helicopters trying to dip low enough to get clearer photos and video to chronicle our predicament. I wonder why they don't attempt to lift any of us to safety. All they do is buzz around like flies on a carcass, filling the sky with a deafening noise that makes my head pound.

The first day people yell and wave at the helicopters, begging to be rescued. After realizing that their presence is meant to record my pain instead of actually doing anything about it, I turn my attention elsewhere. No way am I going to be caught on a news highlight reel with my pain and plight on display for all the world to see. On the second or third day, Coast

Guard helicopters join the news crews in the sky. They actually begin picking people up by lowering baskets for stranded people to climb into and be lifted to safety. Once the Coast Guard arrives, there seems to be a new sense of panic to be one of the lucky few to be plucked from the wreckage of what's left of our homes. People are yelling and waving their arms, vying for the attention of those in the copters. It's a sick sort of competition among terrified people all begging to be noticed and hoping in desperation to be chosen to be rescued.

Late on the third day in the midst of all the noise, heat, and chaos, suddenly the skies empty, and the helicopters disappear. Panic spreads from rooftop to rooftop as we immediately think we've been abandoned. But then a huge airplane lumbers by at low altitude slowly over our heads. I distinctly see the presidential seal of Air Force One and realize they've cleared the airspace so that President Bush could do his own fly-by inspection. As soon as the plane moves past, there is a rush of noise as the copters return, jockeying for position to get footage of the people desperately waving at the president's plane, yelling for help.

Because of all the downed power lines, cars, and debris that choke the flooded streets, rescue airboats can't get close enough to the houses to rescue anyone, so the copters are the first line of defense. After hours in the scorching sun and oppressive heat, I can't take it anymore and go back inside the attic to wait. Nightfall brings some relief from the heat, but New Orleans mosquitos don't care about the devastation. They make their presence felt in painful ways for most of the night. There's no light except for the moon, so at times it's pitch-black, and I can't even see my hand in front of my face.

All of a sudden, the silence of the night is shattered by a deafening whirlwind of noise. The house shakes slightly, search lights crisscross the sky, and it sounds like helicopters, this time larger and louder than the ones we've become accustomed to that carry the news crews. There are shouts and bullhorns and people yelling. It's all completely intelligible in all the chaos. I can't see what's happening; it's just too dark. So I instinctively stay inside the attic, waiting for whatever is going on to pass.

The noise lasts late into the night, and then silence. Just as suddenly as it began, it stops. The next morning, I venture outside to find out what had happened. As my eyes adjust to the bright light and I look around, I realize that no one is there. There are no people on the rooftops. No news copters in the air. No airboats picking their way through the flooded streets. The noise I heard the night before was from the helicopters and boats that had come through and picked up everyone else. Because my house is located away from the other buildings where people had gathered in groups, no one knows I am here.

I have been left behind.

Love Yourself Enough to Trust the Process

Change is an intense process. It shakes you to your core and causes you to question everything you think you know about yourself and others. New situations challenge you in different ways and create opportunities to learn, grow, and develop. The very thing that makes change wonderful is the same thing that makes it seemingly unbearable. The uncertainty you experience can be frustrating and emotional. What do you do when you know that this is good for you, but you still have issues believing it? You love yourself enough to trust the process.

I know you're probably wondering what in the world I mean by that, so let me explain. When you're sick or not feeling well and the doctor prescribes medication that tastes absolutely horrible, what do you do? Ignore the medication because it tastes bad and has some lousy side effects that make you nauseous? NO! You suck it up, take the meds, and follow instructions because you know that even though this may be horrible now, doing this will help you to heal and ultimately feel better. You do what's uncomfortable for a specified period of time because you love yourself enough to trust that what you're doing will ultimately make you better. That's the way it works with change. You have to commit to the process of being uncomfortable now because you trust the process will yield better results for you later.

Even though some change events can leave you feeling devastated (case in point, my Katrina experience), believe that you have what it takes to create new opportunities for growth, development, and success for yourself. This isn't *in spite of* what happens to you, but rather *because of* the process you undertake and the journey you complete. When you embrace the process of change and see it as an opportunity instead of a punishment, you're open to all the benefits that come with participating fully and honestly in the journey.

You can't receive all the benefits of the process if you don't commit to going all in. Embracing change is ultimately an act of self-love. It's loving yourself enough to want to do the work to become the best version of yourself that you can possibly be.

Regret Nothing!

I'm an avid reader. When I was four years old, my cousin used to read Disney fairy tales to me to keep me occupied. Eventually, I started making the connection between the words on the page and the stories that fascinated me. Once I discovered that books and stories were a portal into a whole new world of fantasy and adventure, I was hooked. I read for a variety of purposes, but mostly I read to experience new ways of thinking. I came across a passage in a book entitled *The Choice* by OG Mandino (1984) that I found so impactful in the way it describes our collective battle with change that I wanted to share it here:

> So many of us think ourselves into smallness, into inferiority, by thinking downward. We are held back by too much caution. We are timid about venturing. We are not bold enough. And so we die before we reach middle age, although we will not be lowered into the ground until we pass three score and ten. What happened to the grand dreams of our youth? Suicide. Struck down by our own caution, our own lack of faith in ourselves and our abilities. Opportunities? There were many. But always there was risk. Do we dare? We vacillate. Time hurries by. Opportunities gone. We anguish. The years roll on. Finally, we convince ourselves

that it's too late and settle for cheap imitations of life. We envy the achievers. How lucky they are.
I choose a better way to live!

That passage spoke to me because it sums up perfectly the internal battle that wages within so many of us when it comes to choosing between embracing change to live boldly and living a life of safety and, ultimately, regret.

You think "small" because you fear failure. You doubt your abilities. You don't want to experience pain (again), or you just don't want to work that hard only to be disappointed. You are haunted by the questions and self-doubt ringing in your ears: *What if I fail? What if it doesn't work? What will people say?* Then if whatever you venture out to try doesn't work, you beat yourself up over mistakes and missteps.

If you truly want to live a life fulfilled—a bold life and a happy life—REGRET NOTHING!

"Regret" is defined by *Merriam-Webster.com Dictionary* as "to mourn the loss or death of; to miss very much; to be very sorry for; to experience regret" (accessed October 19, 2020). Most of us operate from a place of pre-regret—overthinking the "what ifs" in our heads to the point that we don't even try. Instead, we play it safe and miss out completely on opportunities and experiences. You can't learn, grow, or progress properly playing it safe.

Have you ever watched a toddler? They freely explore and interact with the world around them to learn and experience new things. Young kids don't *know* to be afraid of things unless they're *taught* to be. In a toddler's world, every experience is fully explored, and they are fully committed to being present in the moment.

What would your life look like if you lived by the "regret nothing!" creed? What would you try? How would you engage and connect? What would you learn? How would you respond to disappointment? How differently would you approach life and living? Every day you have a choice. You, and only you, have to decide how to live each moment. Regret nothing!

Thinking about your path to personal and professional development. Building your career or business. Finding your purpose. Discovering your gifts. Living your life. All of these require effort, engagement, and commitment. But to what end? What does it all mean? Why does it all matter? You have to answer these questions for yourself. Regret nothing!

I would strongly suggest and urge you to think long and hard about what you want your life to feel like each day. Filled with fear, or expectant and excited? Will you dread each experience or explore new possibilities? It's your choice. Make a commitment to yourself. Right here, right now. From this point forward, regret nothing!

Reclaim Your Voice

In the spirit of fully committing to and embracing the process of change, it is important to note that trusting the process is not only about loving yourself and living boldly enough to face each day without pre-regret but also about being true to your voice. To reclaim it. Notice I didn't say to "find" your voice. Using the word "find" implies that your voice is lost or misplaced and that you don't know where it is. Reclaiming your voice means to demand or obtain the return of, to regain possession of, to *rescue from an undesirable state*.

Let that sink in for a moment—to *rescue from an undesirable state*.

When it comes to your voice, quite truthfully, you tend to give it away because of people, situations, trauma, fear, anxiety, and uncertainty. Your "voice" is a representation of who you are at your core. It is you showing up in your full glory as your whole self. When you give away your voice, you give away a piece of who you are. And little by little, you start trading who you are for the approval and acceptance of others.

I grew up as a highly verbal, inquisitive child who learned to read at the age of four. I was extremely active, had an incredible imagination, and questioned everything. When I started first grade, I was already writing sentences and reading short stories. I was excited about going to school because I was SO ready to learn. I used to spend my days reading books to my stuffed animals and couldn't wait to have other kids my age that I could talk to and read with.

My elementary school classroom was a traditional setting with desks arranged in rows and worksheets distributed for us to practice forming the letters of the alphabet. All of the students in my class were expected to complete the worksheets individually and quietly at our desks. My teacher, Mrs. C, would walk up and down the rows passing out the worksheets and then go back to her desk at the front of the classroom to allow us time to complete the assignment. Once we were finished or if we had a question, we would raise our hands and wait to be recognized.

Because we sat in alphabetical order by last name, I ended up sitting toward the end of one of the rows toward the back of the room. Every time Mrs. C gave me my worksheet, I would be finished, out of my seat, and standing next to her to turn it in by the time she had walked back to the front of the classroom. And every single time, once I was finished with my work, I needed something to do. Since Mrs. C told me that I couldn't play with anyone until they had finished their work, I naturally decided to speed things along and started "helping" the other kids with their worksheets.

Mrs. C found herself constantly saying things like, "Keisha, please don't help the other students. They need to learn how to do that on their own." "Keisha, please keep your bottom in your seat while doing your work. You shouldn't be kneeling in your chair." "Keisha, could you please allow some of the other children an opportunity to ask a question or share?" When I received my report card, I had excellent marks in the academic areas. (They literally gave us *E* for Excellent, *S* for Satisfactory, and *U* for Unsatisfactory.)

My behavior grades and the comment section on the back, however, were a completely different story. Each report period was the same. Written in red ink was a series of comments for each grading period that showed a progression of increasing frustration: *"Keisha is a joy to have in class. Please talk to her about doing seatwork." "Keisha loves to help others. Please talk to her about allowing the other students to finish their own work." "Keisha TALKS ENTIRELY TOO MUCH and does not stay in her seat. Please talk to her about this."*

In my young mind, I was doing nothing wrong. I was simply being me. During one lesson, I had once again finished my work before the other kids and had found my way to the front of the classroom where I was "helping" one of my classmates complete their assignment. Mrs. C turned around and saw me, and something snapped. She grabbed me by the arm, dragged me to the front of the classroom, pulled out one of those child-sized chairs, and sat me down in it—hard. She grabbed a roll of duct tape from her desk and proceeded to tape me to the chair. Then in an act of extreme frustration, she paused for a microsecond and—taped—my—mouth—shut.

There was a collective gasp from the rest of the students in the class. There I was, duct taped to a chair with my mouth taped shut, on full display at the front of classroom. I sat there for the remainder of the morning lessons. Mrs. C never looked at me. None of the kids wanted to make eye contact. I squeezed my eyes tightly shut to hold back the tears, but I could feel my cheeks burn with shame. I wanted the floor to swallow me up. I couldn't believe what had happened. There I remained, on display, until it was time to go out for lunch. As the rest of the class lined up to leave, Mrs. C released me from my punishment. She never said a word. I took my place in line quietly and walked out with the rest of the class. I couldn't bring myself to make eye contact with anyone and spent lunch and recess alone. I was humiliated. I was devastated. I couldn't understand why that had happened, and I immediately felt it was somehow because something was "wrong" with me.

The lessons I took from this incident were 1) my voice was "too much"; 2) if I speak out and show up as my full, authentic self, I'll be silenced; and 3) it's NOT okay to be different.

Because of this experience at the age of seven, it took me almost forty years to truly embrace my gifts and reclaim my voice. During that time, I became an advocate for others when their voices were being dismissed and disregarded. Speaking up for them was my way of advocating for myself. But I still wasn't being my *own* advocate. I wasn't fully showing up *for* myself *as* my full self. Every time the opportunity presented itself for me to claim my place in front,

I would shrink back. Whenever I was called upon to speak out, I would fade into the background. In the back of my mind, I still harbored those doubts that my voice was "too much"; I would be silenced, and it's not okay to be different.

Gradually, I had to learn to rediscover and reclaim my voice. Hosting my *Mindset 2 Mastery* podcast is a way of reclaiming my voice. Showing up on stages and leading learning sessions (I don't like the term "training") as my true self is reclaiming my voice. Creating and sharing videos is reclaiming my voice. Assisting others to enhance the levels of engagement, learning, and leadership in their organizations is reclaiming my voice. Guiding and facilitating organizations in the process of equipping their people to embrace and manage change is reclaiming my voice.

For you, what are the ways you're hiding in plain sight? How are you not honoring who you are by remaining silent and flying under the radar? Ask yourself who you are showing up as right now and then describe who you *want* to be. Is there a difference? What needs to happen in order to move you closer to the person you truly are at your core? How do you show up? How are you being real and authentic? How are you honoring your growth, gifts, talents, and abilities?

Ensuring that your personality and authentic self is infused into everything you do is a good start. Being free to share your experiences without fear of judgment or rejection is the goal. Reclaim what is yours and never let it go.

So What Now?

You've traveled with me along a personal journey through the process and steps of change that I hope has opened your eyes to the power of true transformation. This journey is one that I hope that you would take for yourself so that you can be the best possible version of who you were created to be. But more than that, I want you to understand this process so that you can help to support others in their journeys. I want you to recognize the uncertainty and anxiety of the change event. To learn to be empathetic and nurturing during the shift of transformation. To be committed and steadfast during the process of establishing your next normal. I want you to not only understand the process of change but also live it, cherish it, and nurture it in others.

The real value in undertaking this endeavor lies not in what you can accomplish individually, but in what you can do to work with others and contribute collectively. *Change is a personal process that takes place in a collective existence.* No one is an island unto themselves. Whatever affects you impacts me. We are truly connected. Think about the ripple effects that our experiences have on those around us. Our emotional states, old baggage, fears, anxiety, hurt, pain, triggers, and trauma are all felt by those closest to us. It doesn't matter if someone lives in your household or works with you at the office. Whatever you feel and are going through, they feel too. It's time that you recognize, acknowledge, and accept responsibility for your influence and impact on the world around you. It's never just about you—but it does involve you. You are the key. You are the catalyst. You can be the change that you want to see and that others need in the world.

> After the initial shock of realizing that I'm alone, I have to make a decision about what's next. I obviously can't live in my attic under these conditions, but there's nowhere to go, and I certainly don't have enough food or water to last if I'm going to be stuck here for much

longer. I have no idea when or if anyone is coming back to look for me. My mind races as I survey the inside of the attic and try to piece together a plan. After pacing around the short area on the roof back and forth frantically, I realize that I'm not thinking clearly, and panic is starting to creep in.

There's nothing that can be done right now, so I do the only thing I know to do. I pray. I pray for strength, for guidance, and for direction. I pray for the lives of those who have been lost. I pray for those who are afraid and alone. I pray for healing, and I pray for comfort. I pray for us as a city and for the people I know individually. I pray for a sound mind to think clearly, and I pray for a pure heart to avoid bitterness. Most of all, I pray for peace. Peace in the face of adversity. Peace in the midst of calamity. Peace that surpasses all understanding of what I see, what I know, and what I can't understand. Peace as my shield. Peace as my shelter. Peace as my center and foundation to help guide me through what's ahead.

As night approaches, I still don't have any answers. I reflect back on my life and think about the opportunities that I missed, the things that I wish I had done and how I had been looking forward to the work I had lined up with the first client of my new consulting company. Starting this company was my first time doing something that I wanted to do, felt I was born to do, and that I alone controlled. I called the shots. I decided whom to work with and how to proceed. And now, I wasn't sure if I would ever get to finish the work that I had started. But most of all, I wasn't sure if I would get to continue the journey. I wasn't sure if I had used my time on this earth wisely. Was this it? Was this all I had to contribute? Did I really make a mark? Would I be remembered? Did I even matter? What type of impact did I really make? I lie awake in the darkness. Alone with my thoughts.

The next morning begins like the past few since the storm—surrounded by water, awakened by the bites of mosquitos and the suffocating heat. I crawl out of the attic and take a look around. Still no one on the rooftops around me. The sky is empty. No helicopters. No search parties. No one is coming.

Time drags by slowly when there's nothing to do but wait, so I have no idea what time it is or how long I've been sitting there lost in my thoughts. I'm suddenly jerked out of my trance by the sound of a man's voice. He's calling out, "Hello ... is anyone here?" I immediately cry out and give my location. As he rounds the corner, guiding the boat carefully in the alley that's now a channel between my house and my neighbor's, I have never been happier to see another human being in my life! He's in a small fishing boat and is going through the neighborhood to search for survivors in places where the airboats can't reach. Apparently, as I'd thought, the commotion I heard that night was a massive rescue effort. They couldn't pick up everyone and were coming back to round up those who remained from a school nearby. The fishing boat had washed up near his house, so he took it upon himself to go through the neighborhood searching for survivors and bringing them to the school to be rescued. He isn't sure if they are planning to come back beyond the planned trip tomorrow morning, so

96 | FROM TRIAGE TO TRUST

he wants to pick up as many people as possible while there is still daylight.

I eagerly agree to go with him and duck back inside the attic to gather my few belongings. As I stand inside the attic, I take a moment to look around at what had been my home and what I was all but convinced would have become my tomb. I say a word of thanks as I turn and climb down into the boat. We push off and carefully navigate the obstacle course of power lines, debris, and dead bodies to make our way to the school. When we arrive, he hands me off to the others who are already waiting and then sets off again in search of more survivors.

The next day comes and goes, and no rescue copter arrives. No airboat is dispatched. We wait, scanning the sky and posting lookouts in shifts at the windows ready to flag down a passing boat. We hang clothing and other items from the windows to make it clear to anyone passing by that there are people left in the school. As time passes and darkness approaches, we desperately try to hold onto hope. Convincing ourselves and each other that they're coming for us. "They just need more time. Judging from the flooding in our area, there must be a lot of people in need of help, so they just have to work their way back to us. We'll be picked up soon. We just have to be patient. They said they were coming back." These are the things we tell each other. The words we repeat to give ourselves hope. These are the words that we speak out loud to drown out the thoughts that we dare not share. We can see it in each other's eyes—the need to believe, the tenuous hold we have on any small sliver of hope, the shadows of unspoken doubt.

After the second day comes and goes by without any sign of a rescue boat or the promised helicopter, we have to face the possibility that no one is coming for us. At that moment, I have a decision to make: how am I going to navigate this? Being at the school is better than being in the attic, so what now?

There's a total of thirteen of us—ten adults and three children. We have a meeting, and I suggest that every able-bodied adult be given a job or responsibility to help contribute to the smooth running of what has become our small community. Some take charge of cooking, others rotate cleaning duties, and some of the men go out in the fishing boat to find food and look for survivors. I decide to take charge of the children given my background as an educator, and I focus on providing activities for them to keep their minds and hands busy. With my small band of willing students, we scour the school for supplies, make candles, create signs to hang out of the windows, take turns caring for the elderly among us, and have regular "school time" where we write in journals, conduct experiments, read, solve problems, and work on puzzles. We fill the days as much as possible with purposeful activities to keep us from falling into despair or hopelessness.

After another three or four days, as I'm sitting in the window trying to find some semblance of a breeze and looking out for any boats, I notice an airboat passing on another street. I quickly call out and yell for the others to come and join me at the window. We yell, wave, and scream, finally getting their attention so that they change course. The rescue workers pull the boat under the window that I'm practically hanging out of to ask for information. We tell them how many of us there are, how long we think we've been here (the days have started running together), and share that we had been waiting for a rescue copter to return. They radio our location back to base and call for a copter to drop rations and food. It turns out that in the chaos of the massive rescue effort a few nights before, someone forgot to update the rescue map to show that there were still people who needed to be picked up at our location. As a result, no one knew that we were here. They wouldn't have come for us. This boat was on its way to bring water and supplies to a church a few blocks away, and the operator had somehow taken a wrong turn and gotten lost.

A few hours later, a helicopter from the national guard arrives, and we are brought a carton of rations, bottled water, and a box of food. A ranger drops down on a rope from the copter in what looks like a scene out of a movie. He takes a headcount, gets a health update on everyone here, and promises that a copter will arrive at 0600 the next morning to pick us up. After he leaves, we enjoy our meal and talk about what's next. Turns out that some of the men were released from the parish jail when the flooding started, and they're not interested in leaving. There are a few others who have never left the city and are steadfast in their belief that things will get back to normal once the water recedes, so they decide to stay and take their chances. There is no sleep for me tonight. My mind races as I think about what's next. I have no idea what awaits me.

The next morning a coast guard helicopter arrives and lifts the older members of our group up one by one in a small basket to safety. Only four of us can fit in the copter at a time. I'm going with the first group since I've been taking care of the elderly people at the school and they're being transported first. Most of them have medical conditions and have been without their medication, so they've been given priority status. After they've been lifted up, it's my turn. As I'm going up in the basket, I have the opportunity to see for the first time the true depth and range of the effects of the storm. As I travel higher and higher up toward the helicopter, I can see miles in every direction, and all I see is water and destruction. As I take it all in, I can't hold my emotions in any longer and break down in tears.

I'm pulled into the helicopter, and once I'm secured, the pilot and copilot transport us on our journey to the staging area where we will be processed and directed to what's next. As I sit in silence with my thoughts of all that has happened in the past week, I notice the copilot staring at me with a huge grin on his face. We make eye contact, and he asks loudly over the sound of the copter, "Can I take your picture?" while holding up and pointing to his small disposable camera.

Taken aback and thinking about how dirty I feel and how disheveled I must look; I immediately think there's no way I want to be a part of someone's souvenir moment. I jokingly ask him why he wants a photo when, clearly, we don't look our best. He grins even wider and says, "You are the first people I've found alive. I just wanted a reminder that I did make a difference."

~~~~~~~~~~~~~~~~~~~~~~~~~

"Change the mindset.
Master the success."

~~~~~~~~~~~~~~~~~~~~~~~~~

PART II

The Deep Work of Change: Transforming Organizations from the Inside Out

CHAPTER 5

Doing the Deep Work

Creating opportunities for transformation is the deep work of change. Strategic mission statements, plans, protocols, processes, and procedures are usually the focus when people think about organizational change. But the real work—the truly deep, long-lasting work—happens in the discomfort and uncertainty of the process of change. Organizations can only go as far as the people who guide them and work within them. If you want to truly make a difference and create an impact, you have to understand and be committed to the deep work of transforming organizations *from the inside out.*

Organizations react to change the same way that most people do. Why? Because they're made up of people. When you understand and accept that, you'll understand the reason why organizations resist change even when they know it's necessary. It's been said that the only constant is change. So why do people and organizations fear change if it's actually the only thing that's a constant?

I began this book by taking you through a personal process and journey for a very important reason—there can be no change, transformation, or deep work within companies and organizations without equipping people to embrace and manage change personally. In fact, the process of organizational transformation is actually led and sustained by your people. The deep work of organizational change cannot, and should not, occur without them.

How can you grow, learn, and develop truly and fully if you resist change? How can you create dynamic organizations and creative, collaborative spaces and cultures if you resist what's next and hold fast only to what you know?

Picture this: you're in your office, and a coworker knocks on your door before the team meeting and whispers, "Did you hear? There are going to be some *major* changes around here next quarter! I honestly don't know why they're doing this. *We've always done things this way.* Why change now?"

How many times have you heard that conversation or one very close to it? When this is the prevailing attitude among employees, what chance does the organization have of implementing and sustaining long-term change?

The biggest reason people resist change is fear. Fear of being left behind. Fear of uncertainty. Fear that they can't handle new things. Fear of how they'll fit into the next normal. Fear of learning new things. Fear of a loss of security. Fear of failure.

What if you didn't just manage change but embraced it to reinvent yourself, create success, and achieve your organization's goals and outcomes?

In my work with organizations, I do just that. In this section of the book, I'm going to take you on a journey to provide best practices, strategies, tools, and insights to equip you to do the deep work of transformation within your organization.

Use this opportunity to reinvent your organization to become a better version of itself. Even trees change with the seasons. This is your chance to build a solid foundation, so you can thrive in any situation.

Change or Chaos: You Decide

The process of change, when done right, usually involves facing different realities and adapting to them in a systematic, intentional way.

Chaos is change unchecked, unmonitored, and unresolved. Far too many organizations, teams, and people learn to function in chaos because they mistakenly believe they are learning to manage change. They mistakenly see this chaotic environment as being one of innovation and progress where their people are always "on their toes." But when people don't have stability or a foundational set of principles and processes to use in their process of innovation and adaptation, it leads to mistakes, high stress, and burnout. Let's take a look at two scenarios that will paint a better picture of the difference between the two.

Chaos. You walk into work, and there's an email marked "urgent" informing you of new protocols and changes to your team and department—effective immediately. The email includes a checklist of items you must now do to comply with the new regulations. There is no designated person to ask for guidance or field questions. There were no previous discussions around changes that were being considered, and in fact, your team just completed an audit and update of the old protocols that this email now says are being replaced.

Change. Your team has been in talks with management for the past few months about what outcomes are expected, how current initiatives are performing, what the new vision looks like in action, and what is needed to make it happen. Your audit and update recommendations of the current protocols have been shared, and the group has a Slack channel devoted to ideas for innovation where you share ideas and possible solutions. Initial changes to the protocols were discussed and agreed upon by the team with dates of implementation publicized, and impacted work groups have been notified. A subcommittee has been created to provide support, answer questions, and monitor the transition.

Which scenario would you prefer? That's an easy answer. Now, which one do you usually see in organizations? The way most organizations deal with and approach change is the same way that most people manage change. *In order for change to be effective and successful, it has to be systemic, strategic, and sustainable.* What most organizations actually do is create chaos with processes and mandates that are haphazard, reactionary, and short-lived. *The actions of your organization will always mirror that of the mindset of the people who make the decisions.*

Keep in mind when companies and organizations design systems and processes (i.e., recruiting, vetting, hiring, onboarding, mentoring, selection, promotion, merit, etc.), whatever mental models and subconscious biases are inherent in the people who design these systems will show up in the systems. You cannot create long-term systemic change in organizations without leading the process of true cultural and mental transformation in your people. Change the mindset. Master the success.

Is It Real Change or Just Show-and-Tell?

When I was an elementary school teacher (in one of my many past lives), my first graders loved show-and-tell. Once a month, they got to bring in something that was special to them that they could show the rest of the class and tell them about. While it was great for the kids to share things that were special to them, there were some limitations for the audience: no one else got to experience whatever was described for themselves; no one else could touch whatever you were showing, and they definitely couldn't own it or take it home; and the audience had to take your word for it that it was indeed as great or special as you described or thought it was. In organizations faced with change, leaders sometimes resort to a version of show-and-tell instead of implementing real long-term change.

In the show-and-tell version of change, leaders may show you *examples* of what "can be" but never give you an opportunity to participate, engage, or have input into creating that vision or making it a reality. They tell you what to do but don't lead alongside you. Instead, they leave instructions (maybe) and may outline procedures or a list of outcomes, but they don't walk through the process with you.

On the flip side, real, sustainable change is based on shared experiences where you learn together to grow together. Input from various groups in the organization are sought after and thoughtfully considered—usually by a cross section of people who will be impacted by the changes. The collaborative process is enhanced through developing a shared bond and an overall culture of trust. Real change becomes a part of the organization's culture. It's a shared belief that "this is who we are" instead of "this is what we do." This change in mindset and shift in the way of thinking leads to focused action and changes in behavior. People within this type of environment develop a new lens through which they filter their decision-making and that defines what they see, think, and do.

Real change is sustainable. When organizations focus on the transformative process of change, they create learning organizations that follow a belief system rooted in an approach summarized by a quote of unknown origin but often attributed to Benjamin Franklin: "Tell me and I forget; teach me and I may remember; involve me and I learn." Sustainable change goes beyond the specific players and people are who are involved in the change process to creating a culture where change is so embedded that you can change the players and the change remains. New people coming into the organization are welcomed, involved in the process, and become acclimated easily. The result of this type of change process is the creation of a next normal that is supported and sustained by everyone in the organization. This type of real change impacts and influences the organization's engagement, learning, and leadership.

Are You Solving Problems or Designing Solutions?

You can't create sustainable change without shared understanding and collaborative action. Language is important in shaping the way you think. The way you think determines how you act. When organizations charge their people with tasks related to creating outcomes, it's important to note whether you are being asked to solve problems or design solutions. The process of change requires a specific approach to create sustainable success. The language you use is integral to how your people approach change and create and achieve specific outcomes.

Let's start with the fundamentals. If you want to understand what you're asking of your people, begin with the meaning of the words that you're using to describe the task and desired results. Take a look at the meaning of these words according to *Merriam-Webster.com Dictionary* (all accessed October 19, 2020):

- *Solve*: to find a solution, explanation, or answer for.

- *Problem*: a question raised for inquiry, consideration, or solution; an intricate, unsettled question; a source of perplexity, distress, or vexation; difficulty in understanding or accepting.
- *Solution*: an action or process of solving a problem; an answer to a problem; a bringing or coming to an end or into a state of discontinuity.
- *Design*: to create, fashion, execute, or construct according to plan; to conceive and plan out in the mind; to have as a purpose; to devise a specific function or end.

Solving problems is a microfocus on a specific situation or issue that is a "source of perplexity, distress, or vexation." The very language around the term "problem" creates a negative connotation in the minds of people. When teams focus on the "problem" in front of them, they develop a more limited point of view, creating tunnel vision that shuts out anything but the source of their distress, which then impacts what they see as being possible. The process of change, however, requires a more open and flexible view of the *potential* inherent in the possibilities. Teams focused on solving problems go in with a much narrower view and therefore may miss the opportunities present in the process of transformation.

On the other hand, developing teams that focus on designing solutions creates an environment that cultivates macro, big-picture thinking and more creative and inclusive practices. Solving problems is more reactionary to what is in front of them, while solution design is more proactive and empowering with an eye toward what can be created. *The way teams see the work has a profound effect on the way they approach the work.*

Cultivating an environment that is conducive to development and long-term sustainable outcomes requires a shift in the way your teams think and act. That change begins with the language you use to frame expectations and directions that teams are given. The more language you use that empowers teams, encourages them to think outside of the box, and supports initiative and big-picture thinking, the better your teams will respond. Providing encouragement and guidance and cultivating an environment that encourages and challenges people to ask questions and take time to reflect will equip them to apply these best practices in other situations. Teams who are comfortable with the process of being uncomfortable are more innovative, think more comprehensively, and create new approaches that address multiple issues.

The world around us changes rapidly and requires agile teams, not just to react to the changes but also to create a new course of action and to anticipate and navigate the shifts that are to come. Reactive teams wait for the problem (and sometimes the answer) to be defined for them. Proactive teams are creative, empowered, and use ingenuity to expand their thinking and the possibilities. They not only consider what's in front of them but also examine other influences and best practices from a variety of viewpoints and sources of information. Let's look at this distinction in action:

The Setting

The meeting hasn't started yet, but there is a definite nervous energy in the room. Rumors have been circulating that if the latest issues aren't addressed—and quickly— some changes will be made. Suddenly, all heads turn to the front of the room as the regional manager enters and begins to speak.

Scenario #1

The regional manager says, "Good morning, everyone. As you undoubtedly have already heard, there are a series of serious problems within this division that need to be addressed quickly and efficiently. You are in this room because you have been identified as the core of our project team. You are being tasked with identifying the best way to solve the problems that have been identified by our leadership, developing action steps to correct these problems, and sharing the findings and new protocols with the employees who will be directly impacted. You will be briefed shortly on the specifics, your roles, and the timeframe in which this needs to be done."

Scenario #2

The regional manager says, "Hello, team. I know the rumors have been flying fast and furiously, so I wanted to provide some clarification for you, then answer any questions that you may have before we discuss the best approach to take and any steps moving forward.

"Yes, it's true. The division hasn't been performing as hoped and expected. We have some ideas as to what may be causing the discrepancy, and we'll share that information once we get to the planning phase, but our goal is to also get your insights and ideas as we move through this process.

"You're here in this room because of your expertise and experience with the specific issues, as well as anything connected to them. Keep in mind that this isn't the final team. As you review the data, please feel free to recommend anyone else that you feel needs to be in this room. We are looking for people who need to be a part of this process to identify the specific areas of focus and design the most effective and sustainable solution.

"Let's begin by sharing what we know thus far."

Which scenario do you believe would yield the best long-term results? How would you feel as a team member in each of these rooms? Which room or scenario would create an atmosphere most conducive to open-ended creative thinking and collaboration?

When you use limiting language, establish a punitive atmosphere, create a high-pressure environment, and create a feeling of each person being on an island, you inhibit the process of change and create barriers to the true transformation and shift that needs to happen for your people and organization to be successful. Organizations set the stage through the language they use. This directly impacts the mindset and actions of your people. If you want to create organizations where people are open to and receptive to change, growth, and success, then your organization needs to feature language that speaks to that and procedures that support it on an ongoing basis—*not just in a crisis.*

If managed correctly, the process of change can be fulfilling and create opportunities to transform and uplift your people and organization. Laying the correct foundation requires a focus on the intersection of engagement, learning, and leadership.

~~~~~~~~~~

"You have to be
comfortable in your
own skin in order to be
open to sharing who
you are with others."

~~~~~~~~~~

CHAPTER 6

Engagement

"**E**mployee engagement" describes the relationship that employees have with their organizations. It includes the extent to which they feel passionate about their jobs, how committed they are to the organization, and how much effort they put into their work. Engagement is influenced by how well the goals of the organization are aligned with the day-to-day work and goals of the employees. When organizations create inclusive environments where employees feel connected, appreciated, and aligned with their vision and direction, engagement is high, and the change process is easier to facilitate.

Annual polling on employee engagement by Gallup typically reports 65–70 percent of employees feeling disengaged in their positions. *Organizations don't work if people don't feel connected, supported, and valued.* It is important to create a culture of trust that will empower and engage your people while also preparing them to work together collaboratively. Employee engagement practices within organizations include attention to diversity, equity, and inclusion initiatives and issues; empowering and supporting employees to show up fully and authentically as their "whole" selves; providing safe spaces to encourage

open, transparent dialog; and supporting a culture that
is collaborative.

Moving from "Us" to "We"

Human beings are all individuals who at their core
just want to connect and belong. As a result, individuals
tend to align themselves with others who are similar in
some way—department or job title, geographic location,
seniority, race, gender, ability, interests, etc. The key to
employee engagement is moving individual employees
from thinking of themselves as being an "us" (part of a
singular group within the organization) to being a member
of the "we" (the organization as a whole). This shift may
seem minor, but it is an important foundational distinction
that can shape the entire culture of your organization.

Vignette

Your company has been tasked with designing a
solution for a very high-profile, high-impact problem
that threatens profitability, market share position, and
public perception. To tackle the issue, the COO has
pulled together a "task force" of experts from different
departments and divisions to work as a team.

The team members have been selected based
on their areas of expertise, professional experiences,
and level of organizational influence. Even though
the team is focused on designing a solution to a
common problem, as individuals they can't be more
different. They're a mixture of different cultures,
races, gender identity, political beliefs, leadership
style, solution-design approach, learning styles, and
communication preferences.

You have been named team lead. How do you bring this diverse team together in order to build consensus and create a culture of trust, collaboration, and cooperation—oh and, yes, actually design a solution to the problem?

Here are some points to consider. Remember that human beings are all individuals who have a need to belong. The key is to celebrate the individuals while inviting them to join and be a part of the collective group. Reaffirm their contributions and importance to the group—their gifts, talents, and abilities—that make them valued members of the team. Encourage them to show up as their whole, authentic selves. Acknowledge their differences but frame them as strengths to demonstrate how they are equipped to support each other. Encourage transparency and open communication to lessen misunderstandings and support opportunities for sharing and collaboration.

Emphasize the "we" (which is inclusive) versus the "us" (which is exclusive). "Us" is a grouping construct created naturally based on similarities (i.e., where you grew up, what you look like, what culture you belong to, etc.) that separates you from others. "We" is an inclusive action based on forming connections. To create the "we," you have to shift their thinking from being exclusive (us as insiders versus them as outsiders) to being welcoming and inclusive, namely the "we" as community. Create new ways of highlighting the similarities that extend across traditional grouping tendencies, such as shared interests or skills. If possible, change assigned roles to give different people an opportunity to operate outside of their naturally perceived "us/them" construct.

Think of it this way. When someone marries into a family, they are welcomed as a new addition, but during the course of family gatherings, there will always be conversations where stories and anecdotes around shared history and past experiences are told. As the "newbie," you're not going to know the backstory, and because you weren't there when it happened, there's bound to be a slight feeling of being left out—even if unintentional. On the other hand, if you're moving into a new community, when you meet your neighbors for the first time, you're both approaching it looking to build consensus, common ground, and make connections. You don't focus on what separates you but look at ways to connect, and there is more effort made to be inclusive. You begin with a shared common ground of living in the same community. This is the same approach that you want to cultivate with your teams.

Provide an opportunity to create a collective shared vision where everyone participates in the process. *An externally provided vision is a mandate. An internally created vision is a motivator.* To create the inclusive "we," individuals need to form a new reason to bond and connect. A shared vision that *they* create as a group encourages trust and a collective effort. Make sure the gifts, talents, and abilities of each team member are connected to the overall vision, mission, or goal of the team/organization (not aligned solely with a specific subgroup) and play a role in designing a solution for the problem and achieving the outcome. Above all, use the language of "we" consistently. Talk about the team. Praise group effort. Encourage collaboration and foster a culture of understanding. Be an active part of the "we." As a leader/facilitator, it's important for you to serve as a model as well as to participate in the process. *You can't mandate a culture of collaboration; you have to collectively create and facilitate it from within.*

Are You Showing Up as Your Whole Self?

If you want to do the deep work of transformation, you have to show up fully as your whole self. As I mentioned in part I, change is transformational. You can't be committed to the process of change and transformation and require or expect others to be transparent if you are not willing to do the same work yourself. While people are usually slightly more open to the prospect of being transparent during personal change and transformational processes, that's usually not the case when it comes to professional settings.

For some reason, there has traditionally been this divide between who we are at home and who we are at work. An extreme pivot in the way we work during the COVID-19 global pandemic changed all of that. For the first time, whole organizations were required to shift significant portions of their workforces to remote and virtual settings. People were participating in video conferencing and team calls where it was impossible to separate and hide their home lives from their work lives. COVID-19 shifted the way we thought about work-life balance and what it meant to show up fully as your whole self. People weren't "working from home." They were at home during a global pandemic trying to work. The focus shifted from centering and prioritizing "work" to centering the person. This is exactly where the focus needs to be if you want to do the deep work of change within your organization.

As this shift was taking place, the video of George Floyd's murder was circulated, sparking protests around the world decrying discrimination and systemic racism and highlighting the existence of microaggressions against Black people. Companies and organizations had to step up to address issues of diversity, inclusion, equity, and belonging. Hiring practices were called into question as employees started to share their stories of being marginalized, discriminated against, diminished, and dismissed. COVID-19 and Black Lives Matter protests forced organizations to begin the process of changing their approaches not only to how they treated their people but also to how they connected with and engaged them.

To be truly engaged and connected, team members must feel as if they can be fully themselves. Creating a culture of belonging encourages your people to tear down barriers and find ways of building bridges. Truly collaborative and supportive environments are those where the work has been done and the foundation laid to establish trust and opportunities for people to connect without fear of rejection. If you want your people to embrace change, you have to provide safe spaces for them to bring their whole selves to work and be welcomed with open arms. You can't dictate culture. You have to provide models and opportunities to create it. This means you have to be observant, accessible, and willing to walk alongside them in the process. You can't lead anyone in this unless you are willing and able to put yourself in their shoes and see things from their perspectives.

Vignette

You are the newest member of a project team tasked with managing and monitoring client experience. The rest of the team is fairly diverse with regards to the number of men and women and representatives of various races, ages, and years of experience. You start to notice quite a bit of small talk and friendly banter among some of the group during meetings—mostly around weekend activities and hobbies. Although you are asked questions that show they're inviting you to participate, you either hesitate or decline, even though you share the same interests. You can't seem to shake the voice in your head of your elders, mentors, and supervisors admonishing you in past situations to keep your personal life out of the professional. According to them, if you want to be successful, keep your head down and just do your job.

After several weeks, you notice the rest of the team has stopped making an effort to include you. Whenever you're around, the conversations shift to the business at hand since that's the only time you engage with the rest of the group. You begin to feel more isolated and are afraid that you might lose your spot on the team. What do you do?

There are three main issues to be addressed in this scenario: 1) lack of cohesiveness as a team; 2) the team member feeling ostracized and separate; and 3) the team member beginning to appear one-dimensional. What would you advise this team member to do? How would you encourage them to shift their thinking about what it means to connect and show up fully as their whole self?

When people have been conditioned to do things the traditional way before joining your organization (or even if that's the way it had been done where you are now and you want to make a change), it's important to walk them through the process of shifting their thinking. This requires a reframing of their role and the importance of recentering their perspective. *They are not their role/position; they are a person (use their name) doing the work of a role/position.*

People do business with and form relationships with people they *know* and like. You have to be known and let yourself be seen. Because teams are multidimensional and multifunctional, you need to show different sides of who you are to develop trust and to learn to collaborate. Responsibilities shift during the course of your work process, so you have to know your team, and they have to know you fully in order for you all to work better together. Your participation in the company golf tournament or discussing your common interests helps to paint a fuller picture of who you are all around. Those situations showcase different skills and abilities that may not be apparent in a traditional work environment. Showing up as your whole self adds to the diversity, gifts, talents, and abilities of your team and your organization.

Open up. Participate in conversations. That's how people make connections, break down stereotypes, and shatter preconceived notions. Be authentic. You have to be comfortable in your *own* skin in order to be open to sharing who you are with others. When you can be open with others, you can help to create a more inclusive, collaborative, team environment.

You can't fight to be included or foster a sense of inclusion for others if you're hiding in plain sight. Building rapport and relationships takes effort, consistency, and vulnerability. Gone are the days when you had to be two different people—one at work and one at home. The preference now is to be personably professional. Teams are now working together more closely. People have to adapt to new ways of thinking and communicating to design solutions for complex problems and produce results in a fast-paced, ever-changing environment. Teams *have* to embrace their differences to rise above them, build rapport, and be successful.

Transformation cannot occur if there are silos and a disconnect between your people. The traditional models of work actually *don't* help in this process. Be the catalyst. Spark the change. Embrace the shift and lead the way by example. You and your teams will be better because of it.

The Art of Communication

Whenever you're faced with change events, transformation, and the process of discovering and creating your next normal, it's natural that some disagreements will arise in the way things should be handled or approached within your team and organization. There will also be difficult but necessary conversations about the mission, vision, direction, and moral compass of the company and team. Especially in light of social issues that come into play within the organizational cultural dynamic, you need to be prepared to have difficult conversations and to facilitate respectful dialog with people in your circle and sphere of influence around racism, discrimination, diversity, inclusion, equity, and belonging.

It doesn't matter if the conversations are around performance, layoffs, restructuring, mergers, acquisition, downsizing, unconscious bias, race, or a shift in vision—there are some core principles that you should adopt that will enable you to create a culture of respect and facilitate open dialog among your people.

Communication is about an exchange of information between parties. That means it's a give *and* take. Each person gives cues, verbal and nonverbal. Each person receives or takes information and interprets and processes it based on their own context, experiences, perceptions, and preconceived notions. It's not so much what you *say* as what is *heard*. Most people listen to respond instead of listening to understand. If you find yourself thinking about what you're going to say next while someone is talking, then you're not focused on understanding; you're more interested in talking.

If you want to foster a trusting environment where people feel comfortable sharing their thoughts, ideas, and perspectives, and contribute openly and honestly, then you should practice sound listening techniques. Pay close attention to what someone is saying. Repeat what they said to make sure you understood and received the message correctly. Ask probing questions to gain more insight, acquire additional information, and build upon your understanding and their thoughts. Remember that your mind creates meaning by building upon things that you already know, so connect what they're communicating to something you already know and understand to help facilitate conversations and vice versa. Above all, learn to embrace the silence. You don't have to fill every pause with words. Allow people the time and space to ponder, reflect, and review what was said. Communication is a two-way street. Make sure all parties are contributing and receiving from the exchange.

Whatever you do to help create opportunities for open dialog and promote understanding in your individual interactions is what you should be fostering with your team, so they can implement the same practices with others. *Navigating, embracing, managing, and succeeding through the process of change requires an atmosphere of trust, vulnerability, and transparency.* Your team must be equipped to communicate effectively to be successful. That is a nonnegotiable of the process.

Having Difficult Conversations

Organizations are made up of people. People are diverse. Different backgrounds, interests, cultures, languages, political and religious affiliations and beliefs, education, goals, aspirations—there are so many distinctions to consider when working with and leading your teams. While diversity is a benefit that creates opportunities for varying thoughts, approaches, gifts, talents, abilities, and experiences to be added to the table, it can also create situations that can become divisive if you're not careful. Whenever people work in close proximity to each other, they are bound to disagree about things. In fact, you would hope to have differing perspectives within your team and organization to enable you to consider all the possible outcomes in your work. But what happens when the issues of society begin to impact the working environment of your organization?

As I mentioned, this book is being written during a global pandemic (COVID-19) at the same time that protests are being held in support of Black Lives Matter and against police brutality and systemic racism. This was the perfect storm that plunged companies and organizations into the middle of a societal issue that they may have overlooked in the past. But because the video footage of George Floyd's murder was undeniable in its graphic nature, Black employees and allies began to speak out, asking for change. Companies quickly realized that this was not an issue where they could afford to remain silent or stand by and not take action. As such, many companies created opportunities for difficult conversations about racism, discrimination, diversity, inclusion, equity, and belonging. In my work with companies and organizations to facilitate these conversations, I've created a framework that has been successful, and I want to share three foundational points of that with you.

- *Listen, don't hear*. Hearing is physical. It only involves whether your ears work properly to receive the tones and sounds around you. Listening is intentional. It involves taking the tones and sounds you hear and translating those into meaning. Creating safe spaces for people to feel comfortable sharing begins first and foremost with a commitment to listening.

- *Think outside of your own box.* Everyone has their own "box" of perspectives, experiences, biases, and beliefs. When listening, the key is to avoid framing the information in such a way as to change it to fit your own "box" of perspectives and immediately creating an argument or push back to reject it. Instead, use the items in your "box" to connect new information to things you already know and create a new understanding. Step outside of your box to envision what it would be like to *walk in someone else's shoes.* Keep in mind that your journey is traveled according to *your* map. Different routes can be taken to arrive at the same destination. Just because someone's journey or route is not the same as yours doesn't make it any less valuable or valid. Your way is not the only way or even the best way; it's just a different way.

- *Shift from "explaining" to "learning."* When engaged in conversations that are emotional, confrontational, or challenging, it's easy to fall into "explanation mode" where you feel the need to explain your position or opinion. When you explain, you come from a sense of right versus wrong and are more interested in defending or presenting information. You're not open to new insights or perspectives, and you're certainly not seeking to engage or connect. When you seek to learn, you focus on trying to understand and are more open to receiving information, reflecting on it and thinking about ways it can be integrated into the way you think and what you do.

Difficult conversations are hard because they're uncomfortable. They pull us out of our normal way of thinking about things because they usually involve topics that require us to face unpleasant truths and emotional topics or that challenge our beliefs. The process of change *requires* difficult conversations. *If you're ever going to be open to doing the deep work of change and transformation, you have to face falsehoods that you thought were truths; uncover and expose shortcomings and that you thought were strengths; and be willing to admit that change is not only necessary but also required in areas that you thought were permanent foundations.*

When you are open to accepting the process of having difficult conversations, you are open to experiencing the truth of transformation. Being willing to face being uninformed, misinformed, or just plain "wrong" and then committing to the process of changing for the better takes a tremendous amount of self-awareness, vulnerability, and transparency. The deep work of change requires us to put our emotions aside, put our preconceived notions under a microscope, and shine a bright light onto the things that have been hidden in the dark. Traveling this road together makes all the difference when your team or organization is facing hard changes. It is much easier for your organization to weather the storm of change as a collaborative, supportive unit than it is being fractured and dysfunctional. The choice is easy. Face some discomfort now so that you can create and enjoy long-lasting success later.

Overall, when it comes to fostering engagement within your organization, you want to create an atmosphere of trust, collaboration, inclusion, and belonging. Your approach to engagement, diversity, equity, inclusion, and belonging is one that should be ingrained into the fabric of who you are as an organization, not relegated to a checklist of actions to take or protocols to implement. The lens through which your organization sees the world and its place in it needs to factor in the ways in which your employees are supported, included, celebrated, and engaged, not only because doing so is good business but also because your employees are representative of the world outside. They are the pulse of social consciousness and issues. They represent what the public is concerned about and wants. They are the bridge between your organization and the world.

"Growth is a process.
Learning is constant.
Development is
a requirement."

Chapter 7

Learning

For change to happen successfully, all organizations should be learning organizations. If your people aren't placed in positions where they're able to learn, grow, and develop, then you're doing them and yourself a disservice. Gone are the days when people within your companies were expected to be unthinking robots, simply carrying out mundane tasks. In today's world, companies and the people who work within them need to be agile, critical thinkers, strategic planners, leaders, and change agents.

Transforming your organization into a learning organization doesn't mean that you're scheduling nonstop training sessions and workshops. What it does mean, however, is that you're shifting the mindset and approach in the way the organization thinks about and supports learning, growth, and development. This chapter will outline some essential elements that you should consider implementing to support your team's growth. You need to see things from their perspective if you want to create systems and support that will be beneficial to them and what they need. (If you're reading this book as a member of the team instead of the leader, then take these suggestions and present them to your supervisor, manager, or leader.)

Are You Really Committed to Their Growth?

Growth is a process. Learning is constant. Development is a requirement. When companies are committed to the growth of their employees, they make a point to provide opportunities to encourage and support long-term learning, growth, and development. This includes opportunities for individualized study and learning, mentorship, collaboration, application, and reflection. Companies and organizations can no longer offer one-size-fits-all professional development programs that consist of a list of preselected webinars. Your people are individuals. They learn differently, have various interests and learning styles, and need individualized paths to achieve their goals.

So-called independent study or growth programs where employees are provided with or allowed to select their goals and then left to their own devices to map out a plan to get there are good to a point. Information is static. Knowledge is dynamic. It does them no good to be left alone to find the information and not be able to actively apply it in a supportive environment that provides guidance and feedback. Even if you have employees who are self-starters, you can't leave them alone on an island to manage their own process of growth. Since the organization is going to be the beneficiary of their newfound skills and expanded thinking abilities, it's only fair that the organization assist them in the process of developing those abilities and skills.

Growth and development cannot occur in a vacuum. Learning requires interaction and engagement. You need connection and opportunities to apply what you're learning. You need to question what you're discovering and to be mentored by others who are more experienced. You need safe spaces to test new theories, to innovate based on new information, and to learn from and reflect upon any failures.

It's obvious from what I just described that most organizations are not set up this way. So what does commitment to growth actually look like?

- *Creating a Professional Growth Plan.* Each person has their own, individualized Professional Growth Plan (PGP) that is created jointly by their Personal Growth Team (usually the person, their mentor, their supervisor, and a colleague). If you fail to plan, you plan to fail. The PGP outlines the specific goals, outcomes, and behaviors that you want to see. It includes items that are specific, measurable, attainable, relevant, and timebound. When creating the PGP, it's important to note that there needs to be a connection between the goals and outcomes identified on the plan and the roles and responsibilities that the person fills within the organization. If there is an interest to move to another area or position, then that has to be noted as well. Instances where plans such as this (or close versions of it) have been used as a last resort to document protocols and steps taken before an employee is terminated are why people have shunned their use over time. PGPs are a wonderful tool—if used properly. Remember that PGPs are NOT to be used as ammunition to show low-performing employees the door. Designed and used well, they can be a great source of learning, innovation, and advancement for your people.

- *Providing opportunities to explore and engage.* People are social beings. They learn best in social settings. Providing opportunities for your people to question, test, experiment, and share their findings with other people is a core component of a learning organization. It's not enough to simply go through the process or action steps of completing a task or activity; you have to be able to discuss the process with others. How does this apply in other areas or situations? How does this change if we do X? What does this mean to what we want to do next? Questions like these are ways not only to explore the results that you're seeing but also to engage with others in meaningful ways to help support learning and growth across the team and organization. These discussions shouldn't be limited to people within teams or specific departments, divisions, or functions. Providing opportunities for exploration and engagement across various groups within the organization is a valuable opportunity to understand the effects across the organization. This can create opportunities for innovation and solution design that may not have been considered or thought needed otherwise.

- *Offering feedback.* Far too often, feedback is limited to performance reviews, evaluations, or corrective action in many organizations. It's hard to know what to do or what direction you should be moving in if you don't receive any ongoing feedback about your process and your progress. This includes critiques, recommendations, peer reviews, focusing questions and examples, or insights that are applicable to the topic and area of focus. I can't tell you how many times I've heard people provide feedback that added absolutely no value to a situation nor gave the recipient any solid direction of what to do next. It's not enough to feel the need to say something. It's more important to say the *right* thing. When in doubt, ask yourself, "What would this person need to know that would help them to learn, develop, and grow?" If you're not sure, then that means you need to learn more about the person in front of you to understand how they learn, what motivates them, and how they need to receive instruction and direction. Feedback is always focused on creating opportunities for continued growth and learning. It's not a weapon, and it's not meant to diminish, dismiss, or marginalize your people.

- *Reflecting and Resetting.* This is a step that is often overlooked. In order for you to experience true learning, growth, and development, you must have time to reflect and reset. It's a natural tendency for people to believe that they must always be actively doing something if they're committed to growth. After all, if you're not constantly learning or applying something new, then you're not making any progress, right? Nope. In addition to the action of learning, discovering, growing, and exploring, you need time to reflect and reset. This gives you an opportunity to think deeply about what you have discovered. You're able to think about changes, adaptions, and revisions that may be necessary in order to make your new knowledge more applicable and equip you for greater success. In this way, the process of learning, growing, and developing becomes a living, breathing, dynamic one in which you are constantly able to challenge what you are learning and expand your understanding of how things work in the world.

- *Assessing and evaluating.* The final step in the process is to set aside time to assess your process and evaluate your progress. Most times when training programs are implemented, there is an evaluation that tests the outcomes of your learning. But true assessment and evaluation are designed not only to ask questions regarding your retention of concepts and information that you have been exposed to during a training or workshop, but also to determine your ability to apply the information and the outcomes that you achieve as a result. Assessing your process involves reflecting upon the steps that you take during your journey of learning. Evaluating the progress you have made through your learning and development journey helps to determine how you have applied the new information you have received. You must do both in order to gain a true picture of your growth and development.

A commitment to growth requires a shift in thinking. The focus will no longer be on isolated instances of workshops or training. Instead a holistic approach will be created to include learning sessions, application of knowledge, group discovery sessions, focused feedback, and opportunities for assessment and evaluation. This approach will be a fluid one, responsive to the needs of your people, the nuances of new information, necessary changes and demonstrated advancement. By creating an environment supportive of growth, organizations are able to empower their people and ensure their success.

Don't Challenge—Question!

As you make the shift to creating learning-focused organizations, it's important to revisit how you think about questioning. For organizations focused on growth, learning, and development, it's important to encourage questioning as a necessary part of promoting innovation and stimulating thinking. If you want to create organizations that are open to transformation, it's important that your people become comfortable with the concept of asking questions. Notice that I didn't say "challenging"; I specifically said "questioning." The difference between questioning and challenging lies in the intent. To "challenge" something creates an adversarial attitude where most people will think they're out to prove a point or prove something to be wrong. Whereas encouraging your people to ask questions sets the stage for inquiry, innovation. and leads to solution design.

Picture this: Your team is sitting in a last-minute meeting to receive information about a new process that's being implemented across your department. You were one of the team members who advised *against* using the new process during the initial review period. As the presenter begins to outline the process to everyone, it's apparent that there are several things that aren't clear to you, so you raise your hand to ask a question. As your hand goes up, you catch the worried look from one of your colleagues and pause. How do you frame your question so that they don't think you're challenging the presenter or just being disagreeable?

Questioning is an art form. Asking the right questions is key if you want to create a culture of learning, growth, exploration, and innovation. Used properly, questioning is a way to check for understanding, expand the conversation, gain new knowledge, open the door for insights and breakthroughs, and set the stage or lay the foundation for learning. *There is no such thing as a stupid question, but there is such a thing as a badly formed one.* Determining the purpose of the question is the key to determining how it needs to be asked.

Good questioning is an integral part of the process of transformation. When you ask the right questions, you open up the opportunity for exploration. Avoid closed questions with yes or no answers, those that are leading or assumption-focused, ones that close down the inquiry conversation, and statements disguised as questions. Good questions are open-ended and thought-provoking, and they expand the conversation, encourage people to go deeper, and open up opportunities for new insights. Some examples of good questions include:

- What is it about this that makes you say that?
- How does this influence or affect that?
- What have we not considered before?
- How else can we look at this?
- What led you to this conclusion?

Stay away from questions that start with "why." The answer to "why" is always "because." Instead, reframe the question in such a way as to create reflection and encourage shared ideas.

Learning organizations that focus on solution design, growth, innovation, and development encourage and facilitate sound questioning among their teams. The process of change requires you to ask good questions. You cannot learn and transform if you cannot master the art of asking good questions. Take some time to think about how you can go beyond the surface in your discussions and interactions. There is so much more to be explored if you just open yourself up to the possibilities inherent in asking who, what, how, and when. Make a commitment to ask the right questions, so your organization can navigate change more effectively by being process focused and discovery purposed.

What Were You Thinking?

In creating a culture of learning, growth, and development, it's not enough to ask the right types of questions and encourage open dialogue. You must also think about the way you're thinking. *Truly transformative work is reflective work.* Metacognition is an awareness and understanding of your own thought process. True growth and change come not just by doing things differently but also by changing the way you *think* so that you can *be* and act differently.

What were you thinking?! Hearing that phrase usually conjures up images of being chastised or reprimanded and feelings of shame or embarrassment. As soon as those words wash over you, you immediately want to disappear or go back in time to undo whatever it was that you just did to elicit that response. Instead, what if you heard, *"Oh my goodness! What an interesting approach? Can you tell me—what were you thinking?"*

Completely different situation isn't it? The way that you think about the process of thinking informs your process of learning, growth, and development. Metacognition is thinking about thinking, knowing about knowing, and being aware of one's awareness. Reflection is an *active* process that requires you to be aware of yourself both from the outside and the inside. This process enables you to navigate change events, fully embrace the process of transformation, and be more open to the possibilities of creating the next normal. If you want to create opportunities for sustained change and success, you need to become a master of your mind. What you think and how you think guide every facet of your growth and development. The more in tune you are with your process of thinking and arriving at conclusions, the better equipped you'll be for success.

It's Not Failure—You're Learning!

The way you think impacts the way you see opportunities and obstacles. When you embrace new ways of thinking and understand the process of how you think, you're able to shift your perspective to create more successful outcomes. Perhaps the number one obstacle to exploration, innovation, and learning is the fear of failure. When you are afraid of falling short, you automatically try to protect yourself as much as possible. This causes you to pull back instead of leaning in. Embracing and reframing "failure" as opportunities to learn and grow is a key distinction. The process of experimentation is just as important as reflection and observation in the journey of learning and growing.

According to *Merriam-Webster.com Dictionary* (accessed October 19, 2020), failure is defined as "the omission of occurrence or performance; the state or inability to perform a normal function; lack of success; a falling short, deficiency; deterioration; decay." Learning is defined as "knowledge or skill acquired by instruction or study; modification of a behavioral tendency by experience."

Fear of failure leads to risk aversion where you don't try anything new unless you are absolutely certain that it will work or be successful. But if you only try things that you already *know* will definitely work, where's the creativity? Where's the innovation? How do you create anything that has never existed if you only do what is already certain?

Think of a child learning to walk or talk for the first time. He or she falls several times and makes several mistakes. They don't place their feet properly and lose their balance over and over again, falling each time. They make "baby sounds" as they try to figure out how to pronounce new words and phrases. When the child makes a "mistake" (explained in simple terms as not performing the act perfectly), you don't berate them or shame them. Instead, you offer encouragement, gentle correction, and modeling of the desired way of performing the act, so they can learn.

Unfortunately, as you get older, there's less opportunity for experimentation. Less encouragement, less creativity, less questioning, less exploration, and less support mean less opportunity for true learning. If you want to create opportunities for success, then create opportunities and environments that support greater learning. You don't know it all, and you're not expected to be perfect. Things change, so it's up to us to be open to exploring what can be instead of holding onto the comfort and predictability of what is. Embrace the opportunity to create something new. Transformation, learning, growth, and innovation require it.

So how do you create a culture that supports and encourages "failing"? By renaming it. Because the word "failure" has so many negative connotations, it's important to reframe the process as innovation, exploring, reflecting, trial and error, or any other terms that speak to the atmosphere of growth that you want to encourage, rather than stoking the fear that holds people back. There is no learning without risk. There is no development and growth without vulnerability and transparency. Create a culture and community within your teams and organization that thrive on supporting people through their process of exploration, growth, and development. The more your people grow, the better and more successful your organization will be over time.

CHAPTER 8

Leadership

When preparing an organization for change, "leadership development" is perhaps the #1 request for training and professional development topics. But what does "leadership development" actually mean? Usually, these types of sessions are focused on management skills—productivity, process, decision-making, resource allocation, and talent scheduling. Instead of management skills, what's really needed to do the deep work of transformation and equip organizations to embrace and manage change is to create a culture of leadership.

Culture includes customs, attitudes, and behaviors. Within a culture of leadership, everyone leads. Leadership is not something that is left to a chosen few. The vision is shared, understood, and embraced. Collective vision leads to collective action. Accountability is valued—accountability to both the vision and each other. Within this approach, leadership happens within the entire organization and within each person. While you will still have specific roles and responsibilities that require varying levels of leadership, direction, and responsibility, by and large, the culture of leadership within the organization creates a sense of shared responsibility. This is the key to creating dynamic organizations that embrace and navigate change successfully.

Doing the deep work of transformation within organizations requires leaders who develop other leaders. It is important for you as a leader to extend your influence beyond your immediate reach and your time to create a ripple effect. Leaders are measured by the caliber of leaders they develop, not the caliber of their own leadership. The goal of a leader's legacy is to have a broader impact on society and their organization as a whole even after they are gone.

The Four Cs

Because change doesn't occur in a vacuum, it impacts everyone that you come into contact with on a daily basis. This means your friends, family, community, colleagues, team members, and organization will feel the ripple effects of the change that impacts you. Because you're not an island, you must adopt what I call a "leading from within" approach. This means that you see yourself and conduct yourself as a leader within your sphere of influence.

Crafting a successful approach to a change event requires a different type of leadership. This isn't the time for a top-down or authoritarian approach. Change leadership is leadership from within. It requires the input and support of everyone on the team to create success. When organizations are faced with unexpected events, uncertainty, chaos, and disruption, more often than not, most tend to mishandle the change event entirely. Why is this true, considering how many books, articles, training, and certificate programs are devoted to change management and change leadership? If the answers are readily available, why do we still have issues with creating successful pathways through change to create long-term, sustainable results?

Organizations fail at responding to change events because they fail at the four C's required as a foundation for any change event: clarity, communication, commitment, and consistency. As a leader, when determining your organization's response to change events, you must consider each of these areas and work with your people to create the vision of success and be able to act appropriately to bring it to life.

Clarity. Change events require clarity in message, focus, expectations, action, and accountability. If you are not clear about each of these areas, you set the stage for misunderstanding and wasted time, effort, and resources. People need to have a clear picture of whatever is being asked of them. The uncertainty and discomfort of change events can lead to chaos if you're not careful. Bringing clarity to the process enables you to unite the people on your team and within your organization for a common purpose.

Communication. In addition to clarity, change events require effective communication. You have to communicate where you're going, what needs to be done, what your shared vision is, and the actions that will be prioritized and implemented. Additionally, clear communication ensures that everyone is on the same page as to expectations and responsibilities. Open communication also provides an opportunity for people to share their journey and lend their voices to the process. Yes, there will be times when decisions are made by a leader or team and everyone else has to follow, but the way in which this is handled is critical to creating a culture of collaboration and support. When it comes to communication, transparency and inclusion are key.

Commitment. Change events require commitment to the vision, direction, action, and follow-through for successful outcomes. Commitment and dedication must last beyond the initial threat and continue past the point of initial motivation. Creating a culture of commitment ensures that you and your team will push through when things get uncomfortable or difficult. It means people will go the extra mile and be open to trying different approaches to get the desired result. The level of commitment by you and those on your team is the number one indicator of how successful you will be in navigating change events. You can't pay lip service to change. It is a process that requires all hands on deck.

Consistency. To maintain progress during the process of change, consistency is important. Once a plan of action has been outlined, you have to consistently show up and be prepared to do the work if you want to achieve your vision of success. This means consistency in action, but also consistency in accountability, planning, execution, support, and engagement. You can't build consensus, community, and loyalty without consistency. People need not just hear what you say, but also to see that what you do matches your words. Because change fatigue is a real thing (where people get tired of the process of change), consistency is extremely important. It provides a reason for your team to keep going even when the motivation has long passed. Keep in mind that change is a process. It doesn't happen overnight.

Leadership Is Not an Island

No effective leader is an island. Unfortunately, most people think of leading as an isolated role that requires you to complete a specific list of tasks away and apart from your people. The prevailing notion of leadership is a lonely one where there is great power but little connection to others in the organization. That can't be further from the truth.

Effective, successful leaders are connected, engaged, and a part of the organizational community. To shift this way of thinking, we must debunk some common leadership myths and adopt new approaches that will help you in the process of change while creating a culture of leadership that will ensure success.

The purpose of leadership is not to go before your people; it's to travel with them. As a leader, you facilitate and guide the process by engaging with your people. This includes communicating, collaborating, and crafting a culture conducive to success. Even though you may guide them in showing them the way, you are an active participant in the process and the journey. So much of leadership happens alongside your people, not in front of them.

Leaders cannot—and should not—do everything alone. The process of building a team requires that you delegate through trust. You can't do it all and shouldn't attempt to carry the weight of the world on your shoulders. It is important to trust people to do their jobs, fill their roles, and get out of their way. If you provide clear guidance and everyone is operating from a shared vision and direction, your team should be able to fulfill their responsibilities as needed. This trust empowers your people to adjust, reset, and course correct as necessary to achieve the goals you have all outlined together. Micromanaging creates distrust and erodes confidence. Apathy creates isolation. It is important to provide praise as well as appropriate feedback that guides, motivates, inspires, and provides a sense of competency. People need to feel as if they are capable and up to the task being asked of them. As a leader, you can create a collective feeling of connection that will bring your people together for a common goal and vision.

To build an effective team, you must develop a culture of mutual respect. Collaboration requires trust for your people to be open to other ideas, perspectives, and approaches. As the leader, you may have the final say, but you want to build a culture of inclusion, not apathy within your team. When people feel valued and believe that they can contribute to the process, they are more apt to actively participate in the process of creating success.

Compliance versus Commitment

Those who are tasked with leadership roles are charged with getting things done within the organization. There are two different approaches to achieve this: compliance or commitment. Compliance focuses on managed behavior. If it's not expressed, then it doesn't get done. Employees with a compliance mindset wait for directions instead of taking the initiative. There is a narrow scope to the activities and expectations presented, and if something doesn't fit in the "box," then it's not pursued or considered. The goal of employees within a culture of compliance is to check the boxes, operate within the established parameters, and stay out of trouble. They won't offer additional ideas or insights. They'll shy away from innovation and creativity. Compliance is a wet blanket snuffing out the fire and excitement inherent in outside-the-box thinking.

However, a culture of commitment encourages employees to take the initiative. They are proactive, solution oriented, and focused on the vision and goals of the organization. They don't wait for instructions or directions. They are trusted to identify areas of focus and create action steps. They engage with each other and their leaders to ensure alignment in direction and desired outcomes.

Because they are trusted, they reciprocate that trust. Their goals align with what's best for the company and organization as a whole, and they're constantly seeking new ways to be better. Employees who are committed tend to go above and beyond for the simple fact that they don't view their roles as limited. Everyone is committed to the success of the organization as a whole, which means everyone benefits from that success.

Organizations with a culture of leadership are committed to moving from compliance to commitment. They create an environment where employees are actively involved in and included in the decision-making process. You want to create opportunities for your team to feel as if they are making an impact. This requires both a culture shift and a mindset shift from the traditional approach. Instead of a top-down approach, a belief in the importance of shared decision-making, influence, and responsibility becomes the norm. When people feel valued, included, and important, they become committed to the overall success of the organization. That is what you want to establish in order to ensure long-term, sustainable success.

Leading from Within

I know this may seem like a lot. So how do you put all of this into action?

Let me paint a picture for you: You are a member of a five-person team that reports to a regional manager. Your manager is responsible for giving direction, establishing goals, and ensuring that all the teams are working together to achieve the overall goals. Five different teams in your region report to your regional manager. All the teams are based in different locations. As the teams begins work, there are some issues. You don't receive regular updates. There is overall confusion regarding what to do, and the regional manager spends most of their time talking about things that have already happened (or what didn't happen), but very little time giving direction or feedback that's useful. None of the regional teams communicate with each other. Morale is low, and stress is high. There's talk of a shake-up in the region, and several people are floating the idea of leaving. What do you do?

The main issues in this scenario are lack of direction; lack of clarity, consistency, and communication; and lack of results. To address these issues, leaders must be vocal, visible, and visionary. Vocal leaders provide feedback and communicate expectations. Visible leaders are seen *and* heard. They are present at meetings and provide confidence to their teams. Visionary leaders paint the picture of where you're headed and help you to envision success.

I know what you're thinking. The scenario said that you're a *member* of the team, not the leader of the team. So realistically what can you do? You have to utilize an approach focused on leading from within. Leadership is not only relegated to those with a specific title or role. Anyone who has a vested interest in the success of the team, department, and organization can step up. What does this look like? Using a leading-from-within approach, every team member is positioned as a leader of their own role. They serve as an example to others by being visionary, visible, and vocal about their area of expertise. They connect the dots by doing the research and discovering how what they do individually affects the whole team and organization. They keep this connection in mind while doing their jobs as a way of centering the overall goals and purpose of the organization within their roles. They speak up, ask questions, request meetings, and facilitate group collaboration through communicating with others. They don't wait to be told what to do; they express what they need and want with a focus on spreading the wealth. When one is successful, everyone is successful. This approach takes initiative. It requires commitment, and it must be built on a culture of collaboration and cohesive action.

After leading the teams in implementing these strategies, when revisiting your teams six months later, we see a very different picture. Team members spend more time talking to each other about what needs to be done, how it needs to be done, and its overall impact on the team, region, and organization as a whole. People feel engaged, empowered, and important because they believe that they *matter*, both individually and collectively. Teams are reaching their quarterly goals and have developed a great rapport and sense of camaraderie.

This is not an overnight process. It takes consistency and dedication to achieve results. To begin the process you must create an opportunity for people to join together to achieve a common goal. This takes time, but it can be done. Invite others to join with you and create a "we" approach that shows them what inclusive leadership looks like in action. Change is a process that begins with an event. You don't have to wait to be appointed. You don't have to wait for permission. As a team leader, why can't *you* be the catalyst that sparks that event—that one action—that first step?

CHAPTER 9

Walk the Talk—The Journey Continues

So here we are. It's the end of the book. I can almost guarantee that you still have a lot of questions and are wondering if you can really pull this off. All the things you've learned about change, what it means, what it looks like, and the amount of work that goes into actually doing the deep work of transformation can be overwhelming. I get it. Believe me—there are days when I wish I didn't know what I know. Why? Because then I wouldn't actually have to *do* it of course!

Understanding the process of change means that you now have to actually walk the talk. It's no longer enough for you to talk about change or cosign on surface reactions to change events. No, my friend, you are now fully aware of what change *should* be and how it needs to be embraced, managed, and navigated in order to create success both personally and professionally. *Knowledge is power. It is also a responsibility.*

So what's next? What do you do with all of this information and insight? How do you engage and enlighten others so that they can fully participate knowingly in the process of change to create desired, successful outcomes both personally and professionally? How do you lead from within to engage and empower others to shift their perspective and adjust their behaviors? What do you do to *be* the change event or catalyst that leads others toward the shift of transformation? How can you equip others to take this journey?

In short, when you know better, you do better. Knowing what is expected, required, and needed to embrace and navigate the process of change puts you in a position to do things differently. By doing things differently and sharing your process, thoughts, and knowledge with others, you are able to create ripple effects that extend beyond you. It can seem overwhelming to think that you are responsible for leading a change effort. I completely understand that feeling. But if you really stop to think about it, none of us lives in a vacuum. We are not designed to live our lives separately and apart from others. We are all interconnected, so our actions collectively impact each other, whether we want to admit and accept that or not. *You can't unlearn what you know. You can't go back. You can only move forward, but this time with intention.*

The process of change is a never-ending journey. The more comfortable you become with the process, the more you'll learn, grow, and develop. Accepting change and its role in your life is imperative to being equipped to navigate it successfully. Change happens whether you acknowledge it or not. Wouldn't you rather be equipped to handle it?

When I began this book, I spoke of what change is, what it does, the process, and how it impacts you personally. I shared my own personal journey of change through my Hurricane Katrina experience to illustrate the process of change and what it looked like in action. Then I walked you through the three main areas you need to focus on within your organization to do the deep work of transformation. My purpose in all of this is not just to inform you, but to educate you and equip you to recognize, navigate, embrace, and manage change within your own life and organization. If you take nothing else from this book, I want you to understand that it is impossible to undertake the deep work of transformation if you don't undertake the journey of change for yourself.

Throughout this journey, it's important for you to remember that change doesn't happen overnight. The process and the journey repeat themselves every time there is a new challenge to overcome and a new goal to meet. The steps in the process are always the same, but the way it shows up in your life may look differently based on the details and circumstances.

Change is a nuanced process that requires an individualized approach to every situation. Build upon the foundational framework in this book to equip yourself to learn to navigate the process and to teach others as they travel along their own journeys of change alongside you. The number one requirement is that you have to share what you know with others. You can't assume responsibility for the journey that other people have to travel. You need to share what you know but equip them and hold them responsible to do their *own* work. Sharing your experiences and discussing your challenges is a good place to start. Please, be wary of tendencies to create blanket assumptions or rules about how different people respond to their change journeys. The process can bring people together to support each other, but the nuances and specifics of what the journey looks like for each person should remain an individualized, personal distinction.

My own journey of change during and after Hurricane Katrina caused me to completely shift my thinking about what it meant for things to happen *to* me versus embracing things that happened *around* me. I had to learn not to internalize external events and factors to the point of them impacting my sense of self-worth or my identity negatively. When I was airlifted out of New Orleans, I had lost everything I owned. My only possessions were the clothes on my back and what little I could stuff in an overnight duffle bag. Everything I thought I knew about myself and what made me "me" was questioned and challenged.

I literally had to "prove" who I was to reclaim my identity and obtain a new driver's license. How's that for shaking your foundation of who you are?! ("Yes, we'll be happy to issue a new driver's license, but first you have to prove to me that you are who you say you are. And oh yeah, we're only going to rely on information that we have in a database about you, which may or may not be correct." Sheesh!) I had to fight to be called by my name instead of being referred to as a "Katrina refugee." I had to think about what I wanted my life to look like and what I needed to do to rebuild it, while at the same time fighting other people's perceptions of what they thought I was or would be capable of just because of what they had heard or seen on the news. In addition to reestablishing the physical framework of my life, I was also going through an internal reckoning with myself to determine what and who I wanted to be moving forward. What did this mean for me as a consultant and business owner? What did this mean for me as a person? Who was I going to be? What impact would I make?

Fifteen years have passed since Hurricane Katrina upended my life. Every year that I mark the occasion I am reminded that celebrating this milestone is also a reminder of my experience during and after Hurricane Katrina. I no longer wake up in a cold sweat, heart pounding, and disoriented at the thought that I'm still in the attic listening to the screams of my neighbors. I am finally able to enjoy the sound of thunderstorms without panic attacks. I can finally see myself as a whole person again, not someone who has been haunted by the nightmares and insecurities that come from losing everything you have and being uprooted from what you're familiar with. For me, Katrina has gradually shifted from being my biggest nightmare to becoming a source of inspiration and example of my greatest triumph.

On that sweltering summer day as I stared at the helicopter copilot, I tried to make sense of his words. *"You're the first people we've found alive.''* For some reason, that sentence just did not compute. In a city of hundreds of thousands of people, how can we be the first ones he'd found alive in a week of search and rescue efforts? Could it really have been that bad? My mind raced as I tried to absorb this new information, this new reality. If this storm had claimed the lives of so many, why was I spared? What made me so different and so special? What was I to learn from this? What was I required to do as a result of this?

Living through a harrowing, life-altering event changes you. It changes the way you think about everything—yourself, the world, and your place in it. When you understand the process of change, you can navigate the aftereffects of change events a bit easier. Being armed with information and insights about what to expect creates a life preserver that you can hold onto to keep from drowning in the storm. It doesn't mean you won't be tossed about and bruised a bit in the process, but it does mean that you are all but guaranteed to make it out intact on the other side.

Your defining change event may be something different. It could be an accident, relocating to a new place, a change in your career, family shifts, or even an epiphany that hits you out of nowhere while you're going through the routine of your day. The point is that *what the change event looks like doesn't matter as much as what you do during the change process.* Every event provides us with the opportunity for transformation. Some shifts are small in scope, while others can be life altering. The process remains the same. How are you going to shift? What transformation are you going to undertake? How will you make yourself and those around you better as a result? What will you learn? How will you grow? What will you contribute to the world? How will you make an impact?

It was ten years before I could look at my Katrina experience as a gift. Ten years of being plagued by aftershocks that rocked my confidence and shook my tenuous hold on the new life I had built. Every time a new major change event showed up, I was taken back to that harrowing experience in the attic and the memory of hearing, "*You're the first people we've found alive,*" over and over and over again. Finally, I had to make a decision as to whether I was going to be buffeted about by the winds and storms of change every time something new happened or whether I was going to find a way to navigate this and ride the waves successfully. My journey of reflection, self-study, introspection, and observation has led to this book.

I've always been a strategist in the way that I think and approach things. I've always wondered about the reasons behind things being as they are and what causes certain reactions and responses. I've always been filled with questions and wondered "what if." By dissecting my own process and journey of change, and then applying what I've learned to different areas and situations in my life and in my work with clients, I have created a framework that works.

People don't fear change because of change itself. People fear and resist change because they don't feel equipped to handle the *process* of change. This book is designed to provide a roadmap to equip you in navigating your journey through the process. I hope it is a resource that will equip you and others within your circle of influence not just to survive through change but also to *become* the change that the world desperately needs.

When I started this book, I wrote about the events in the world that were facing us all—a global pandemic in COVID-19, civil unrest sparked by the murder of George Floyd, and a new call for eradication of systemic racism and discrimination practices. Watching people and organizations trying to navigate this storm prompted me to action in writing this book. Not because I feel that I am the self-appointed "Guru of Change" or that I have all the answers, but because I know that I can help others. My journey of change has led me to this place and point in time. I am here because I have something that the world needs. You are reading this book because you have gifts that are important and need to be shared. Your voice needs to be heard. Your efforts are needed.

We are at a place in our lives where it is impossible to live in isolation where our actions don't impact or affect others. The effects of the pandemic and civil unrest have proven that no one is an island. The way that we navigate the process of change creates ripple effects that impact us all. No one is immune from it. No one can ignore it. We must recognize that we are all connected. Because of that connection, it is our responsibility to navigate change events in such a way as to make ourselves and others better. Each of us matters. Each of us is important. Each of us brings our own perspectives, experiences, gifts, talents, and abilities to the table to create something more wonderful.

Learning how to embrace and navigate change is the missing link. Understanding the process of transformation and being able to facilitate that within your own personal journey and throughout the organizations you work within is a game changer. Individually, it is easy to feel helpless and overwhelmed at the prospect of creating change. But when you understand that you are never alone in this, it gives you courage. I'll say it again—we are all connected. When we all commit to doing the deep work of transformation—together—we can create the success that we are capable of and destined to have.

The journey continues. How will you travel it? What will you do differently? How will you commit to creating change for you and spark transformation in those around you? What will be *your* moment of impact?

When you know better, you do better. Now you know. The rest is up to you.

A Final Word

Congratulations! You've made it to the end of the book. Now you're officially at the beginning of your journey.

The funny thing about doing the deep work of transformation is that once you know better, you can't go back to doing things the old way—no matter how much you may want to or try.

I shared this journey with you because I felt compelled to. There was no way I could keep these things to myself after I saw first-hand how many people needed what I had to offer. I don't take writing a book like this lightly. I thought long and hard about it before beginning the process for the simple fact that I wanted it to be right and was determined that it would be worthwhile.

Change is possibly the only constant in our lives, and yet it is the thing that people in general are woefully unprepared to face. When understood and navigated properly, the process of change can lead to wonderful growth and incredible opportunities for learning and development. But unfortunately, proper understanding and navigation is not always the case. And because of that, there are so many missed opportunities to create and live a vision of success both personally and professionally.

This book provided you with a framework to use in creating your own future and walking your path. It allowed you the safety to dig deep and the freedom to dream big. But it is only the beginning. You have uncovered, discovered, and experienced the beginnings of this process for yourself (even if it was living vicariously through reading about my journey). You now know what it feels like and looks like to travel this journey and be open to the shift of transformation. There is no going back.

So what now? What do you do with all of this newfound knowledge and understanding? You make an impact. You create opportunities for change. You cultivate environments where change is welcomed and supported. You stand up and speak out when change is required. You become the change because you own and embrace the journey of change.

The most important thing you can do is to share this with others. Change doesn't occur in a vacuum. Its ripple effect is felt way beyond your immediate circle. But it's up to you to ensure that the ripple effects are good ones and not ones filled with trauma and fear. The process and journey of change unfolds as it will, but the way people interpret, react, and evolve through the process is determined by their thoughts about change. You now have the key to shift mindsets. You now have the knowledge to help others navigate this process. Because you understand, you have to share your gift with others.

Individual change journeys are sometimes thought to be separate from what happens within organizations and companies. You now know nothing can be further from the truth. Organizations and companies are directly impacted by the process of change that their people go through. It's time to embrace that fact—own it and use it to shift your thinking about the way organizations and companies function. It's no longer acceptable to focus on the entity at the expense of its people. Companies and organizations cannot thrive through change without creating a culture that places its people firmly at the center of the process.

This is your charge. It's time to do the deep work of transformation. It's time to become equipped for change. It's time to leave a legacy and create a new vision of success. It's your time. Take the first step. Do it boldly.

Keisha

Change Is a Process That Begins with an Event

"When I found myself sitting in my attic during Hurricane Katrina with rising flood waters rushing into the house, I realized that change was upon me. Five days later when I was airlifted out of New Orleans and placed on a plane going who knows where, I knew I was starting a new chapter. When I arrived at a Red Cross evacuee camp and saw the chaos around me, I knew life would never be the same. When I made the decision to get involved, I felt I could make an impact. When my efforts created successful outcomes, I knew I had found my sweet spot." – Keisha A. Rivers

Keisha A. Rivers survived a harrowing Hurricane Katrina experience to become a successful speaker, change agent, and learning leader. She facilitates successful outcomes by equipping people to embrace, manage, and lead through change. Her work centers on three main areas: engagement, learning, and leadership. Keisha has over fifteen years of experience in the strategic consulting and organizational development space. She works with clients in the consumer goods and services, retail, hospitality, government, and education industries.

An educator at heart, Keisha focuses her approach on teaching clients to understand and create their own unique vision of success. From there they work together to develop the foundation and framework for processes that will create dynamic, inclusive learning communities and empower their teams to take ownership and lead from within. The goal is not just to achieve outcomes and solve problems, but also to equip her clients to sustain their success.

A gifted and engaging international speaker and presenter, Keisha establishes an immediate connection with the audience. In her sessions, participants are transformed from passive recipients of information to active creators of knowledge. Keisha's approach empowers participants to immediately apply concepts and create real-world solutions. She has presented at conferences and led training for companies across the country.

Keisha's educational background includes a bachelor's degree in elementary education from the University of Pennsylvania, a Master of Education in curriculum and instruction with a concentration in leadership and development from the University of New Orleans, and a Women's Entrepreneurship Certificate from Cornell University. She is a certified Talent Optimization Leader, Certified Diversity Professional (CDP), and Certified Diversity Executive (CDE). She is a member of the Network of Executive Women, National Diversity Council, and The Society for Diversity.

Keisha gives back to the community through her 501(c)(3) nonprofit, The KARS Institute for Learning & Collaboration. The organization provides opportunities for collaboration, training, and development to new and emerging community groups and nonprofits. In her spare time, Keisha enjoys traveling, reading, riding her motorcycle, and exploring new ways of learning, growing, and being.

Connect with Me!

Thank you for joining me on this journey. I would love to stay connected with you to support you along your journey and hear about your progress. Please feel free to connect with me via my social media channels listed below, tune in to my *Mindset 2 Mastery* podcast, and by all means reach out to me to talk about ways in which I can assist you and your organization in creating learning opportunities, enhancing engagement, and developing leadership initiatives within your company or organization. Each episode of *Mindset 2 Mastery* offers thirty minutes of actionable insights to help you change your mindset and master your success. New episodes are released twice a week on Wednesdays and Saturdays. Also available wherever you listen to podcasts.

 karsgroup.com

 karsgroup.com/podcast

 karivers

 karsgroupltd

 karsgroupltd

 karsgroupltd

thekarsgroup